RHODES

today and yesterday

A complete guide for travellers
with 145 colour illustrations
and maps

EDITIONS
TOUBI'S
ΕΚΔΟΣΕΙΣ

ATHENS 2011

© Copyright   MICHAEL TOUBIS PUBLICATIONS S.A.
                   Nisiza Karela, Koropi, Attiki, Telephone: +30 210 6029974,
                   Fax: +30 210 6646856, Web Site: http://www.toubis.gr

ISBN: 960-7504-88-7

Contents

Preface

Rhodes really needs no introduction. There are still Greek islands where the visitor who is not armed with a good guide-book will still run the risk of finding himself marooned in the back of beyond with no hope of food or accommodation, but this is hardly the case with Rhodes. The rapid development of mass tourism over the last twenty years or so has at least made sure that the basic facilities are available almost everywhere. What this guide, which we believe is the best of its kind, aims to do is to help the visitor make the most of the island. We hope that the places we describe and the information we give may lead the visitor to discover the beach which suits him perfectly, or take the walk which leads to the most beautiful view — or any one of the millions of things which can make the difference between a good holiday and an absolutely unforgettable one.

We have divided the book into five sections. The first gives an account of the island's history, in a way which we hope is both interesting and informative (and even more importantly, the guidebook which gets its facts wrong is the holiday-makers bane). In the case of an island like Rhodes, with a history stretching back over thousands of years, an awareness of the past can intensify the pleasure to be gained from the present.

Our description of the island is in two parts: the city (old and new) and the tour of the island. This will be useful both for those without transport, but who will certainly want to walk round the old city at some point during their stay, and for those who are able to reach the less accessible parts of the island. The description also gives details of road conditions. Our last two sections go together: details of museums, facilities for sports and games, etc., are followed by a section containing everything the visitor to Rhodes needs to know about Greece in general and Rhodes in particular in order to make the most of his stay and avoid accidentally getting himself into trouble.

In addition to all the above, we have also provided maps of both the town and the whole island and photographs which we are sure will enable this book, by itself, to be a souvenir of a memorable holiday.

Welcome to Rhodes, then!

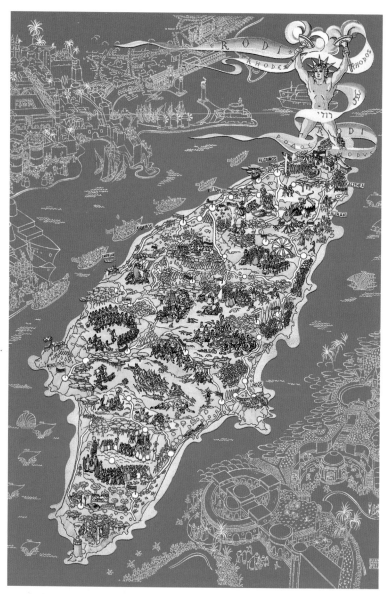

Rhodes is the largest in the Dodecanese, a group of which the following islands are also inhabited: Kastellorizo, Symi, Chalki, Karpathos, Kasos, Tilos, Nisiros, Kos, Kalymnos, Leros, Patmos and Astypalaia. Geological research has shown that the ancient myth of Rhodes emerging from the waters of the Aegean to become the bride of the sun god might not be so far from the truth after all.

GEOGRAPHICAL INTRODUCTION

Rhodes is at the meeting point of three continents - Europe, Asia and Africa. This geographical position has been a contributory factor in the development of flourishing commerce from prehistoric times onwards and in ensuring for the island long periods of prosperity in its three thousand-year history. Its ships were the means by which the cultural achievements of the surrounding peoples were introduced into Rhodes and its own were generously exported. The position of Rhodes on the strategic route between East and West has, however, also been the cause of successive invasions and prolonged oppression.

Rhodes is the largest of a complex of islands in the south eastern Aegean, ranging from the large to the tiny and numbering over 200, known as the Dodecanese. The name means 'twelve islands' and refers to the principal inhabited islands - of which there are, in fact, thirteen. It is believed that some of these islands 'broke away' from the mainland of Asia Minor while others rose from the sea as a result of earthquakes in the remote past. Rhodes probably rose from the sea after some such tremendous upheaval and was also, perhaps, at one stage linked to Asia Minor. This conclusion is supported by the fact that sea shells have been found on its mountain sides.

As it is today, Rhodes has an area of 1,400 square kilometres and is 78 kms in length at its longest point and 38 kms across at its broadest. The terrain is largely mountainous and the land capable of cultivation is confined to strips of coastal plain and small valleys and plateaus. The island's highest mountain is Atavyros (1,215 m.). None of the other mountains attain anything like this height. The coastline consists for the most part of level sandy beaches, interrupted in places by steep cliffs.

The island enjoys a mild climate with adequate rainfall, which accounts for its profuse vegetation. In reality there are only two seasons: spring and summer. After November, when the first rains fall, the ground is carpeted with green and by February Rhodes has become one vast flower garden. May sees the beginning of summer, when the earth gradually takes on a golden colour, until November, when the cycle starts again. On average, Rhodes has 300 days of sunshine a year, while between April and October, the chances of uninterrupted sunshine are virtually one hundred per cent. During that period the temperature is in excess of 25°C. The summer heat is offset by a cooling, and sometimes strong, sea breeze.

The island's limited farmland produces some of the most excellent fruit and vegetables in the Mediterranean. The population, which up to the 1950's was very largely engaged in farming and stockbreeding, then realized that tourism could be more profitable. At the same time, getting to know and looking after visitors from distant lands suits the restless, sociable and hospitable character of the Rhodians. Thus the present population of 100.000 manage to entertain more than 1.250.000 visitors a year - visitors who come to enjoy, with them, the natural beauty of the island and to learn something of its long history.

HISTORY

The Ancient Myths

The origins of Rhodes are connected with a beautiful myth which Pindar and other ancient writers liked to tell in their works. According to this myth, when Zeus defeated the Giants and became master of the earth, he decided to divide it among the gods of Mount Olympus. Helios, the Sun-god, was absent during the casting of lots, and, so the legend goes, «... no one remembered to include him in the draw». When Helios returned from his duties, he complained to Zeus about the injustice done to him. The father of the gods then told him he would cast lots again, but the radiant god did not let him. He only asked Zeus and the other gods to promise that the land which was to rise out of the sea could be his. As he spoke, there slowly emerged from the bottom of the blue sea a beautiful island, profuse with flowers. It was Rhodes, which until then had lain hidden beneath the sea. Brimming with happines, Helios bathed the island with his own radiance and made it the most beautiful in the Aegean Sea.

Another myth attributes the beginnings of Rhodes to the love of Helios for the nymph Rhodos, the daughter of the god of the sea, Poseidon. When Helios saw Rhodos, so the myth goes, he was so taken by her astounding beauty that he made her his wife. They had seven sons and one daughter, Alectrona, who died young. Kerkaphos, one of the sons of Helios and Rhodos, had three children: Kamiros, Ialysos and Lindos. They built a city each in Rhodes, and divided the island among themselves. Some say that the famed island derives its name from the nymph Rhodos.

Others maintain that Rhodes was named after the rose, and this either because the island was abundant in thesea beautiful flowers or because the ancient inhabitants likened its beauty to that of a rose. However, Rhodes was known in ancient times by several other names, among them, Ophioussa, for the many snakes that lived there; Asteria, for its clear blue and starry sky; Makaria, for its arresting beauty; Telchinia, because its first inhabitants were said to be the Telchines; and Atavyria, after its highest mountain, Atavyros.

Prehistory

The history of Rhodes, like that of the rest of Greece, has its beginnings in the dim realms of mythology. In those distant, mythological years the island was inhabited by the Telchines, a strange race of men said to have been endowed with magical powers. The Telchines, said by many to be demons, were also gifted metal workers. It was they who forged Poseidon's trident and Kronos' fearful sickle-shaped sword, the «harpi». Legend also has it that it was the Telchines who cast the first bronze statues of the gods of Olympus. The Telchines were later banished from Rhodes by the Heliads, the children of Helios and the nymph Rhodos. Historically, the first inhabitants of the island are said to have been the Carians, a tribe which came from Asia Minor. The Carians were followed by the Phoenicians, who made Rhodes an important commercial centre. Cadmus founded the first Phoenician colony there and also introduced the first alphabet.

Head of Helios, in the Rhodes Archaeological Museum. The sun-god was worshiped in Rhodes more than any other god - this is not surprising, given his generosity to the island.

However, Rhodes appears in the recorded history of the Eastern Mediterranean from the time when the island was settled by colonists from Minoan Crete. These Minoans lived peacefully on the island for many centuries, until another tribe came to settle in Rhodes. These newcomers were Greek Achaians from Mycenae, Tiryns, Argos and Attica. After they had settled in their new home, some time around 1400 B.C., they founded a powerful state which very soon extended its influence over the neighbouring islands, and a large part of the nearby coast of Asia Minor. Mycenean settlements have been discovered at Ialysos and Kamiros. The Achaians were, in turn, followed some centuries later by the warlike Dorians, who overran Rhodes, after taking possession of the Peloponnese, several Aegean islands, and the southern coast of Asia Minor. In Rhodes they developed Lindos, Ialysos and Kamiros – three cities which, in time, grew immensely in power and wealth. Proof of this greatness lies in the discoveries made in all three cities.

The Rhodians, led by Tlepolemos, the brave son of Hercules, took part in the Trojan War with nine ships. However, the leader of the «pround Rhodians», as they were then known, died in battle together with Sarpidon, before the walls of Troy.

By settling in Rhodes, and other Aegean islands, the Greeks placed themselves near the East and consequently became acquainted with Eastern civilization. Architectural monuments, statues, gold and silver items, and the life of luxury led by the rich leaders of the East had a profound influence on them. Yet these gifted Greeks from southern Greece based their cultural and social patterns on entirely new founda-

Female head (4th cent. B.C., Archaeological Museum, Rhodes).

tions. Not only did Rhodes constitute a singificant cultural centre, but it also developed unprecedented commercial and colonial activities. The fast ships of the Rhodians sailed to almost all parts of the Mediterranean bringing riches and glory back to the mother island. At the same time, the three greatest cities in the island, Kamiros, Ialysos, and Lindos in particular, founded many colonies along the West coast of Asia Minor, Sicily, France, and Spain, from 1000-600 B.C. The most famous of these were Gages, Phasele and Korydala in Lykia; Soloi in Kilikia; Gela and Agraga in Sicily; Parthenope (today's Naples) and Elpiae in Italy; Rhodi (today's Rosa) in Spain, and Gymnesiae in the Balearic islands.

The classical Period

The three cities mentioned above maintained their administrative independence at first, but later united with the other Doric cities Cos, Knidos and Halicarnassus to form the so-called Doric Hexapolis – a federation of six cities, having a political and religious character, whose seat of government was the sanctuary of Apollo Triopios, near Knidos. It seems that the Doric Hexapolis was the result of an effort by the Dorians to found a powerful federation similar to that of the Io-nians, whose federation had been founded earlier, and had its seat at the famous temple of Artemis, in Ephesus.

In the 5th century B.C. Rhodes suffered many changes, brought about by war, and this led to a turn in the fortunes of the island. Eventually it came under the influence of the Persians together with Ionia and the West coast of Asia Minor. When the Persians were in their turn, defeated by the Greeks, they left Rhodes and the island became a member of the Delian League, under the leadership of Athens. Later, during the Peloponnesian War (431-404 B.C.), the Rhodians were at times under the influence of Athens, at others, that of Sparta. Finally, they sided with the Spartans. During the Peloponnesian War, for reasons of greater safety, the Rhodians decided to found a new city by uniting the three largest cities on the island. Thus, on the initiative of Dorieus, the son of the Olympic champion Diagoras, a new capital was established on the north-eastern tip of the island. It was called Rhodes after the island, and its foundation, in 408 B.C., constituted a landmark in the history of the island.

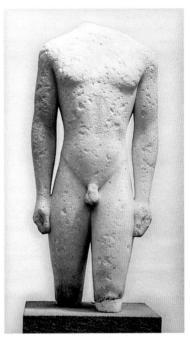

A kouros (male statue) dating from the second half of the 6th century B.C.

The Hellenistic Period: The Years of Prosperity

This beautiful city, like the island itself, came under the influence, sometimes of one or other, of the two great Greek powers, Athens and Sparta, until Macedonia's intentions in that era became clear to all the peoples of the ancient Greek world. The Rhodians lost no time in siding with the Macedonians, and even went as far as allowing them to set up a garrison in their city. Later, during the siege of Tyre, they helped Alexander the Great to conquer it. When Alexander's empire fell to pieces, Rhodes developed close trade and political relations with the Ptolemy Dynasty of Egypt, something which Antigonus,

Left: Athlete head.   *Above: Funerary stele, Kalliaristas (4th cent. B.C.).*

the King of Syria, did not favour because he foresaw an inevitable alliance between Rhodes and Egypt in the war which he intended to declare against the latter. Thus, in the summer of 305 B.C., he sent his son, the famous Demetrius Poliorketes (the "besieger"), to capture the town of Rhodes. Despite their attackers' numerical superiority, the Rhodians managed to resist capture for a whole year, and to force Demetrius to raise his siege. The great general departed from Rhodes in embarrassed haste, leaving behind his famous siege-machines. These were later sold by the Rhodians, andfrom the proceeds they built an imm ense bronze statue of Helios, the famed Colossus. Fol-

lowing the destruction of Tyre, a serious trade rival of Rhodes, the island reached unprecedented heights. The failure of Demetrius to take possession of the island marked the beginning of a new era for Rhodes, during which trade and maritime activities reached their highest peaks, excelling any other state. The Rhodians, wanting to show correct maritime conduct, put into effect the so-called "International Maritime Law of the Rhodians", a code of law which is one of the most important early legal documents in the world. Of this maritime law, Emperor Antoninus was prompted to write with admiration: «I may rule the world, but the Rhodian's law rules the seas».

The Roman Years: The Decline

The intervention of Rome in the affairs of Greece and the Eastern Mediterranean in general became increasingly noticeable from the end of the 3rd century B.C. onwards. The Rhodians did their best to make the most of the way things were turning out, and maintained a friendly stance towards the Romans. However, the Romans were much more interested in restricting the power of the island, and they seized on the Rhodians' reluctance to take part in the Roman war against Perseus, successor of Philip V of Macedon, to declare Delos a free port. This was a deathblow for Rhodian commerce. The harbour taxes fell from 1,000,000 Rhodian drachmas a year, a height which they had reached in recent years and which, at a rate of 2%, mean that total trade in the port must have been of the order of 50,000,000 drachmas, to only 150,000. Forced to its knees, Rhodes was compelled to sign a treaty obliging it to have the same friends and foes as Rome. The agreement brought only disaster for Rhodes, which suffered in both Rome's colonial wars and in its civil strife. Cassius dealt the last blow. After the assassination of Julius Caesar, the Rhodians refused him aid against his enemies, and in his rage he attacked and conquered the town in 42 B.C., wreaking unprecedented havoc. Among other acts of destruction, he carried off some 3,000 of the works of art which adorned the island.

The Middle Ages

Rhodes, lying as a commercial centre between the East and the West, was quick to respond to the new ideas of Christianity. Tradition has it that St Paul preached the new religion at Lindos in 58 A.D. and converted many of the inhabitants. As early as the 1st century, Rhodes had a bishop, Prochoros, later succeeded by Photinos and Euphranoras, who took part in the First Ecumenical Council of Nicea. When the Roman Empire split in two, Rhodes became the capital of the Byzantine eparchy of the islands, but it retained little of its former glory. It followed the destinies and the vicissitudes of the Byzantine Empire, and was often overrun and destroyed by enemies of the state. In 620, for example, it was conquered by the Persians under Chosroes; in 651 the Saracens arrived, and in 807 the city was sacked by Seljuks under Haroun - al - Rashid. At the end of the 12th century, when Alexios I was Emperor of Byzantium, Rhodes was sacked once more, by pirates.

Direct contacts between Rhodes and the West began again in the 11th century. In 1082, the Venetians received the permission of the Emperor to set up a trading station in the port. In 1191, Richard the Lionheart and King Philip of France arrived with a fleet to enlist mercenaries for their crusade.

When the Crusaders conquered Constantinople in 1204, a rich landowner called Leo Gavalas, from the former capital of the Empire, declared himself Despot of Rhodes and was tolerated by the Venetians. The Byzantine emperors took Constantinople back from the Crusaders in 1261, and

Ayios Loukas. Wall painting from the 14th century (Panayia, Kastro).

Rhodes theoretically returned to their control, while in fact remaining in the hands of the Genoese admirals whose fleet lay in its harbour. In 1306, one of the admirals, Vignolo Vignoli, sold Rhodes, Kos and Leros to the Knights of St John of Jerusalem, who gained full control of the island by 1309, in the face of fierce opposition from the local inhabitants.

The Knights of Rhodes

The Order of the Knights of St John was founded as a charitable brotherhood in Jerusalem by merchants from Amalfi, in Italy, who were permanently resident in the Holy City. Later, and especially after 1099, when the Crusaders took Jerusalem, the Order gained in strength and became more of a military organisation un-

der the control and authority of the church. When Jerusalem fell to Saladin, in 1187, the Knights moved to Acre, in northern Palestine. But the eventual total failure of the Crusades drove them out of the area altogether, and brought them as refugees to Cyprus. They stayed only 18 years in Cyprus before moving on to Rhodes. The period during which the Knights ruled in Rhodes was the most bril-

liant in their history. The Knights left imposing evidence of their presence in Rhodes, and gave to the island the particular character it retains to this day, with its impregnable walls, gates, churches, hospitals, Inns and palaces. Their stay in Rhodes lasted 213 years, until 1522, when, on December 29, the last of the Grand Masters, Villiers de l' Isle Adam, was compelled to surrender the island to Suleiman the Magnificent. Needless to stay, it took a siege of six months in the face of strong resistance from the Knights, with the aid of the local inhabitants, before the city could be forced to give itself up.

After the fall of Rhodes, Charles V and the Pope were instrumental in finding the Knights a new home — in Malta. After that time, they were known as the Knights of Malta.

The Organization of the Knights

Arms of the Order

Foulques de Villaret
1310-1319

Hélion de Villeneuve
1319-1346

Dieudonné de Gozon
1346-1353

Pierre de Corneillan
1354-1355

Roger de Pins
1355-1365

Raymond Béranger
1365-1374

The Knights' Order had members of three kinds: the Knights themselves, of whom there were never more than 600, with military duties and a background of descent from a noble family; the serving brothers, whose responsibility was for the sick and whose origin was not necessarily noble; and the chaplains, who conducted the Order's religious services.

The members of the Order came from all the Catholic countries of Europe, and were divided into seven national and linguistic groups, called 'Tongues': of Provence, of Auvergne, of France, of Italy, of England, of Germany and of Spain, which was itself later divided into Aragon and Castille. Each Tongue had its own Inn and was railed by a Bailiff and council.

Supreme command was exercised by the Grand Master, elected by the members of the Order for life, and he was assisted in his tasks by a council, composed of the Bailiffs of each Tongue, which had legislative and disciplinary powers. Latin was the official language for all the Order's documents, and French for spoken communication between members of different Tongues.

The Tongue of France, usually supported by those of Provence and Auvergne, was the most powerful of the groups, and of the 19 Grand Masters who. ruled the Order during their 213 years on Rhodes, 14 were French. This can be seen from a study of the names accompanying the coats-of-arms.

Ph.Villiers de
1521-

Fabrizio del
1513-

Guy de Bla
1512-

Almeric d'A
1505-1

Pierre d'A
1476-

G. B. degli
1467-1

Raymond Z
1461-1

Robert de Juilly
1374-1377

Ferdinand d'Hérédia
1377-1396

Philibert de Naillac
1396-1421

Antoine Fluvian
1421-1437

Jean de Lastic
1437-1454

Jacques de
1454-14

The Turkish siege of Rhodes in 1480 (Miniature by Caursin, National Library, Paris).

Turkish and Italian Occupation

The Turkish occupation of Rhodes was the darkest period in its history, as indeed it was for the whole of Greece. The island was under the control of a Kapudan Pasha (a full Admiral), while the city itself was capital of the Vilayet (Province) of the Aegean and was the seat of the General Administrator.

The Greek inhabitants of the city were forced to leave the walled town and settle outside it, forming new suburbs which they called 'marasia'. But the Turks were never able to attain complete dominance over the island, and the Turkish part of the population was always a small minority. The Greeks had little difficulty in gaining control of trade and commerce, sending their many merchant vessels far afield. During those dark days of foreign occupation, many towns –and especially Lindos– were able to flourish thanks to their trading in foodstuffs, clothing, silverware, household utensils and perfumes. Lindos also developed as an early semi-industrial centre.

Turkish occupation of the Dodecanese lasted until 1912. In that year, the Italians, with the help of the Greek inhabitants, occupied the island, and at first treated the local residents well. There were hopes of a speedy union with Greece. But the rise of Fascism in Italy led to more expansionist policies, and Italy denied Rhodes the right to self- determination. This was the signal for resistance on the part of the Greek population to begin, and it was answered in the most oppressive manner by the Italian occupation authorities. After the defeat of the Axis powers, Rhodes and the other Dodecanese islands came un-

der British military administration until March 7, 1948, when the Greek flag was finally raised over the Governor's Palace.

ΤΡΗΣ — ΕΙΣ

Interior courtyard of Government House.
The Greek Plag was raised here in March, 1948.

Literature

Apart from its great achievements in commerce and shipping, Rhodes also enjoyed cultural prominence. After the 3rd century B.C., especially, it was an important centre of culture and the arts, constituting a veritable seat of learning to which not only Rhodians, but also young men from all parts of the known world came to study. Distinguished Romans, among them Cicero, Julius Caesar, Lucretius, Pompey, Tiberius and Cassius, came to Rhodes to learn the art of rhetoric, and also to study philosophy. Peisandros from Kamiros «distinguished himself in epic poetry, and in his famous work, «Herakleia», he praises the achievements and the virtues of the popular mythical hero, Herakles. Antagoras, also an epic poet from the city of Rhodes, wrote the epic poem «Thebais» and epigrams, of which, however, only one is extant.

The Alexandrian poet Apollonios (295-215 B.C.), known as Apollonios the Rhodian, lived and wrote his works in Rhodes. He was the greatest epic poet of the Alexandrian period. Of his poems, the most widely appreciated is the «Argonautica», which tells of the adventures of the Argonauts in 5835 lines. In the «Argonautica», which is outstanding for its polished epigrammatic elegance and wise sayings, the great poet brings in many mythological events and adventures which greatly appealed to the people of those longgone eras. Apollonios was imitated by the Romans Valerius Flaccus and Terentius Varro Atacinus.

Of the philosophers, the Lindian Cleobouline was pre-eminent, and, during the period of the island's greatest heights it was the Stoic philosopher Panaetius. Mention should also be made here of one of the great philosophers of Rhodes, Cleoboulos,

Ayios Loukas (Byzantine icon).

Black-figured Attican hydria. Archaeological Museum, Rhodes.

the son of Evagoras. He was born and lived in Lindos in the 7th century B.C. He was a wise law-giver and shrewd politician who governed Lindos for forty years. The ancients ranked him foremost among the leading philosophers of Greece. To Cleoboulos are attributed many proverbs, among them: «Moderation in all things», «Restrain all sensuous pleasure»; «Mind maketh a leader»; «Always do right», and «Be pleasing of tongue».

Prominent Rhodian historians were, among others, Polyzelos who wrote, as did Ergeias, a history of Rhodes; Zenon, Antisthenis, Poseidonios, Kallixenos, Sossikratis, and others of whose works little remains. Rhodes prided itself on ist School of Rhetoric, which was founded in 324 B.C., by the Athenian orator, Aeschines. Its fame was widespread, and it was frequented by students from the whole of the Mediterranean, especially Rome. Famous Romans, a few of whom we have already mentioned above, were taught the secrets of the juridical art in the School of Rhodes. Among the famous orators of that era were Molon, Apollonios, Poseidonios, Menekles and Archelaos. With respect to Molon, the great Cicero had this to say: «I came to Rhodes to attend lessons in rhetoric, taught by Molon. He is a gifted orator and an excellent writer, and his criticisms are always given with grace. He teaches with wisdom, and his success is deservedly great».

Ancient theatre on Monte Smith hill.

The Arts

Alongside culture Rhodes showed great success in the Arts. Sculptors, painters and pottery makers produced works which still astound us with their quality and number. Of the **sculptors**, the most famous were Chares, Philiskos, Aristonidas, the brothers Apollonios and Tauriskos, and, lastly, Agesander, Athenodorus, and Polydorus. Chares, a Lindian and a student of Lysippos, created the famous Colossus of Rhodes, one of the Seven Wonders of the ancient world.

Philiskos made statues of Apollo, Leto, Artemis and the Muses. Aristonidas built a bronze statue of the grieving Athamas, who in a moment of madness killed his son, Learchos. The brothers Apollonios and Tauriskos were not Rhodians, but had lived most of their lives on the island. They produced the celebrated composition of the Farnese Bull, a replica of which can be seen today in the Museum of Naples.

Agesander, Athinodorus and Polydorus created many sculptured masterpieces, of which the most famous (a work produced by all three) is «Laocoon» – a composition which represents the punishment of Laocoon, Apollo's priest. The hapless Laocoon, together with his children, was punished for showing disrespect to the god by being condemned to die in the deadly grip of two great snakes which the god had called up from the sea. This famous group was taken to Rome in the 1st cehtury A.D. and discovered in 1506 in the Golden House of Nero in Rome. Pliny, who mentions the sculpture, thought it the most supreme work of sculpture or painting which human hands had ever produced, and even today it is regarded as one of the hief masterpieces of Greek art. **Painting** was also important in Rhodes. Many of the sculptors, such as Aristonidas, Tauriskos and Philiskos, were also painters. But the greatest of them all, and one of the most outstanding painters of all ancient Greece, was Protogenes, who was conceded by his contemporary Apelles to be as good if not better than himself. His only criticism was that Protogenes had a tendency to put in too much detail, which spoiled the grace of his works. Among his outstanting works were Ialysos with his hunting dog, a Resting Satyr, an imaginary portrait of Tlepolemus, etc., while his famous painting of the two Attican triremes, Paralos and Ammonias, were on display at the Propylaea of the Acropolis in Athens.

Pottery-making was also an important part of the cultural life of | Rhodes, and the products of the island were known all over the ancient world. Even as early as the Mycenean period (15th - 12th c B.C.) fine pottery was being produced on the island. Some of this has been found in tombs at Ialysos and Kamiros, and shows scenes from the world of nature and the sea. But Rhodian pottery was at its height during the 7th and 6th centuries B.C., classic examples being the Fikelloura pots (they take their name from the site near Kamiros where they were found). The normal style of ornamentation was a combination of geometrical designs and themes from nature.

Reproduction of the Colossus.

The Colossus

The name of the Colossus of Rhodes is familiar to everyone. Its history begins with the siege of Demetrios Poliorketes, successor of Alexander the Great, in 305 B.C. With the money they raised from the sale of Demetrios' siege machinery, which he had left behind when he withdrew, the Rhodians decided to express their pride in their great victory by building a triumphal statue of their favourite god, Helios. The task was assigned to the sculptor Chares of Lindos, a pupil of Lysippos himself, and twelve years (from 304 to 292 B.C.) were needed to finish it. The Colossus was

regarded as one of the seven wonders of the world and a masterpiece of art and engineering, but we lack reliable information about its appearance and its site. An inscription found near the palace of the Grand Masters allows us to calculate its height at about 31 metres. But most people envisage it along the lines portrayed (from imagination) by the French traveller Rottiers in 1826.

It is said that Chares cast the bronze limbs of the statue on the spot, one at a time, using huge heaps of earth, and moving upwards from level to level, rather as one would build a house. The old myth, on which Rottiers based his drawing, that the statue stood across the entrance to the harbour and that incoming ships sailed between its legs, must, reluctantly, be abandoned. Today we can be sure that it stood on land –apart from anything else, the way in which it was constructed would have dictated that– and that the most likely spot for it to have stood was the courtyard of the Temple of Helios, which lay close to the palace of the Grand Masters.

However, the statue was only a nine-day wonder, or, to be more accurate, a 66 - year wonder. A violent earthquake in 226 B.C. broke its knees and sent it to the ground. The Rhodians, afraid of some curse, did not dare to replace it, and it lay where it had fallen for many centuries. At last, in 653 A.D., Arab pirates under Moabiah who were raiding in the area carried the bronze parts to the mainland opposite and sold them to a Jewish merchant. It is said that 900 camels were needed to transport it. But the legend was so closely linked to the name of Rhodes that for centuries afterwards both Greeks and Europeans referred to the people of Rhodes as «Colossans».

THE CITY OF RHODES

The city of Rhodes, with its 45,000 inhabitants, stands on the same site as the ancient city, construction of which began in 408 B.C. The town thus has a history stretching back over 2,400 years, and monuments from every period can be found within its bounds.

The ancient city was rather larger than the present city. To the South, the walls reach as far as the hills which cut off the triangle of flat ground in the North from the rest of the island. Indeed, some of these hills, such as Monte Smith, were inside the walls. The area enclosed by the walls has been estimated at 700 hectares, while the area of the medieval city or Old City is only 48 hectares. The population of the ancient city during its period of greatest fame and power, in the 3rd and 2nd centuries B.C., must have been about 80,000. Rhodes had not one acropolis, but two — one on Monte Smith and another, smaller, on the site of the Palace of the Knights.

The layout of the ancient city was also different to that of the modern town. It was built in the Hippoda-mian manner: that is, around a number of wide streets in a grid system, running East-West and North-South. There is a theory that the ancient city was planned by the famous Miletian architect Hippodamus himself, but this would appear to be mistaken. Whoever its planner was, Rhodes was the subject of great admiration in the ancient world. As Strabo says,

«We cannot tell of any other city that is its equal, much less its superior».

Rhodes today has to offer an impressive variety of colours and forms, its marvellous beaches, big modern buildings, picturesque neighbourhoods, imposing medieval edifices and Turkish minarets are all swamped in greenery. In the town itself, the streets are lined with trees. Vegetation grows up even as far as the walls of the Castle, and the numerous palm trees hint at the tropical. For many, the best approach to Rhodes is from the sea, from which can be seen the medieval city towering over the harbour, with its biscuit-coloured walls, towers, bastions and battlements. Behind it, the domes and minarets of Turkish mosques. Those who arrive in Rhodes by air, as do most visitors, and thus miss this wonderful experience, can make up for it by taking a trip on one of the many small boats operating out of | Mandraki harbour.

Tourist development on the island in the last thirty years has been almost unprecedented. Along with the money flowing into the island in the form of remissions from emigrant workers, it has contributed to a spate of building activity which is far from dying out. Hotels, restaurants, tavernas, night clubs and shops can be numbered in hundreds, and from April to October the city is an international tourist centre in which the foreigners more or less outnumber the locals.

The tour of the town which follows treats separately the Old Town, which is within the Knights' walls, and the New Town.

RHODES: THE OLD CITY

1. Gate of Freedom
2. St. Paul's Gate
3. Naillac Tower
4. Art Gallery
5. Temple of Aphrodite
6. Arsenal Gate
7. Ionian and Popular Bank
8. Archaeological Institute (Armeria)
9. Museum of Folk-Art
10. Inn of Auvergne
11. Our Lady of the Castle
12. Inn of England
13. Archaeological Museum of Rhodes
   (The Knight's Hospital)
14. Inn of Italy
15. Small Palace
16. Turkish Garden and Fountain
17. Inn of France
18. Chapel of the Tongue of France
19. Chaplain of the Tongue of France
20. Inn of Provence
21. Inn of Spain
22. Loggia of St. John
23. Palace of the Grand Masters
24. Gate of St. Anthony
25. D' Amboise Gate
26. Clock Tower
27. Suleiman Mosque
28. Kurmale - Mendresse
29. Turkish Library
30. St. Paraskevi
31. Moustafa Mosque and Turkish Baths
32. Theatre of the Old City
33. St. Fanourios
34. Redjep - Pasha Mosque
35. Aga Mosque
36. "Kastellania"
37. Marine Gate
38. Palace of the Admirals
39. Our Lady of the City
40. Ibrahim - Pasha Mosque
41. Dolapli Cami
42. St. George Tower
43. St. Mary Tower
44. St. Athanasios Tower
45. Koskinou Gate
46. Gate of Italy

The Medieval Town - The Castle

The visitor should not be misled by the term 'medieval town' into thinking that what he will see is a ruined and deserted city, such as Mystras in the Southern Peloponnese. The Old Town of Rhodes is a bustling neighbourhood of some 6,000 people, who live and work in the same buildings in which the Knights of St John lived six centuries ago; as a living monument to the past it must be nearly unique in Europe, if not the world. Even the visitor whose stay in Rhodes is for no more than a few hours should not neglect to walk round it.

The Old Town continues today to be divided into the two parts which made it up in the time of the Knights: the northern part, which was the internal fortress of the Knights, known as the Castello or Collachium, and which contained the official buildings; and the larger southern part, called the Chora, where the Greeks, the Europeans who were not members of the Order, and the Jews lived. These two parts of the town were separated by a wall running approximately parallel to the line of Odós Sokratous, the old Bazaar. During the years of Turkish occupation, the Greeks were expelled from the Old Town, which was the exclusive province of Turks and Jews. Greeks were allowed to enter only during daytime, and those who were caught in the old town after dark were liable to be beheaded.

Note: "Pili" "Platia" "Odos" mean Gate, Square, Street respectively. Names are spelt as they will be found on street and road signs.

Left: platia symis, with the ruins of the temple of Aphrodite and the Freedom Gate.

The Castle of the Knights (Collachium)

Coming up from Mandraki harbour, we enter through the Gate of Freedom,(Pili Eleftherias) in Symi Square (Platia Symis). The Gate was opened in 1924 by the Italians, who looked on themselves as liberators of the island from the Turks. Immediately opposite are the ruins of a **Temple of Aphrodite**, dating from the 3rd century B.C., one of the few ancient remains to be found in the old town. Behind the temple is the **Inn of the Tongue of Auvergne**, built in1507. Note the outside staircase leading up the front of the building which is a purely Aegean architectural feature, owing nothing to Western influence.

The Inn is used today as government offices. To the left, Arsenal Gate leads to the commercial port. Platia Symis is also known as Arsenal Square, as it was believed that the Knights had shipyards there (the word 'arsenal' is derived from the Arabic word for a shipyard). The building on the right houses the **Municipal Art Gallery**.

From here the street climbs slightly to **Platia Argyrokastrou**, a pretty spot with a fine fountain in its centre. Its base, which is an early Christian font, was found by Italian archaeologists in the church of St. Irene near the village of Arnitha. The pile of can-nonballs near the fountain, and the other piles to be seen here and there in the Old Town, were collected for the defence of Rhodes during the Turkish siege of 1522. Platia Argyrokastrou also boasts one of the oldest buildings in the Castle — the Armeria, built in the 14th century, probably by Grand Master Roger de Pins, whose escutcheon can be seen on the left hand side of the building. Its similarities to the Hospital of the Knights (now the Museum) lead scholars to believe that this was the first building used as a Hospital. Later, it was used by the Turks as an armoury (armeria).

Right: this font was used by the Christian inhabitants of the village Arnida some 1500 years ago. Now it adorns platia Argyrokastrou.

To the left as we look at the Armeria, which today houses the Institute of History and Archaeology, is the **Museum of FolkArt**.

We continue, under an arch, and come out in front of the church of **Our Lady of the Castle**, which was the Knights' Cathedral. It stands at the beginning of the Street of the Knights. In 1523, the Turks converted the church into a mosque (the Enterum Mosque) and the bell-tower, which no longer stands, became a minaret. The interior, however, was left as it was. It is possible that the original structure of the church was Byzantine; estimates of its age range from the 11th to the 13th century.

Immediately after the church of Our Lady of the Castle is Museum Square, (Platia Mousiou) with the Inn of the Tongue of England and the Knights' Hospital. The **Inn of the Tongue of England** is on the left, on the corner of the Square and an alley running down to the port. The building was reconstructed in 1919 in its original position and in the same style as the old structure, which dated from 1443 and was destroyed in the mid-19th century.

The **Knights' Hospital** stands on the right as we enter the square. It is in perfect condition, and is obviously suitable for the initial purpose of the Order, which was to give hospitality and care to pilgrims in need of assistance in the Holy Land, and later to the Crusaders. This large and imposing edifice, which houses the **Archaeological Museum**, (see p.87) is probably the most important monument left by the Knights in the City. Building began in 1440 under Grand Master de Lastic and was finished in 1484 by Grand Master d' Aubusson. Much of the stone and other building materials was taken from the Roman building on the site of which the Hospital stands. On the ground floor, arched entries to the right and left of the main entrance lead to storehouses, which are now used as shops. A similar entry approximately in the centre of the building is the main way into the building; there are carved decorations. Directly above the entrance is a three-sided obtrusion, part of the chapel in the Great Hall on the upper floor. This is the only break in the otherwise unrelieved severity of the frontage of the building. The entrance leads us through an arch into an inner courtyard, surrounded on all sides by a two-storey arcade with low arches. The upper floor is reached by a wide staircase in the south-east corner of the courtyard. The eastern side of this upper floor (facing the square) is occupied by the infirmary ward of the hospital, which was capable of housing about 100 patients. Half-way along the ward is the Gothic chapel, part of which protrudes, as we have seen, over the entrance. The remaining sides of the upper floor were presumably used by the nursing staff. Now we return by Platia Mousiou and enter the **Street of the Knights** (Odós Ippotón). This was the main street in the Collachium, and is perhaps the most outstanding medieval street to be seen anywhere in Europe. Its chief feature is the degree of its preservation and its freedom from elements of a different age. During the early years of the Turkish occupation, the barracks of the occupying forces were brought here. Later, Turkish families were installed, and they added wooden balconies to the front of the buildings, spoiling the harmony of the original architectural conception.

Ippoton Street, a classic example of the coexistence of past and present in Rhodes.

The earlier form was later restored by Italian archaeologists. At first sight, the buildings may seem austere and plain; but even a brief walk will suffice to discover the multitude of different forms and styles of detail. The street is approximately 200m long and 6m wide, and it leads up to the Palace of the Grand Masters. To the right and left stand the Inns of the various Tongues.

As we enter the Street of the Knights, the first building on our left is the north side of the Hospital. To the right, a medieval building houses the Commercial Bank of Greece. This is followed by the **Inn of the Tongue of Italy**, finished in 1519 by the Italian Master Fabrizio del Carreto, whose escutcheon can be seen in the centre of the frontage. Next to this is a **small palace** bearing the coats-of-arms of the French Masters Aimerie d' Amboise and Villiers de l' Isle Adam. Although it cannot be verified with any certainty, it seems that this was the residence of Villiers, the Master who defended Rhodes during the Turkish siege in 1522 and was entrusted with the grim duty of handing over the city to the Turks.

Opposite this palace is the original main entrance to the Hospital. After this, behind an iron gate, is a shady garden with a Turkish fountain, whose running water is the only sound to break the complete silence which reigns there. The Catalan and Aragonese style of a gateway which has survived among the ruins would seem to indicate that the building which stood there was Spanish.

Almost opposite the garden is the **Inn of the Tongue of France**, the most highly decorated of all the Knightly buildings and among the most attrac-tive. It is definitely worth more than just a hasty visit. It was built by the Grand Masters d' Aubusson and d' Amboise at the end of the 15th cen-tury or the beginning of the 16th, and I bears their coats-of-arms on the front I along with the emblem of the Order and the escutcheon of Villiers' de l' Isle Adam. Next to it stands the **Chapel of the Tongue of France**, with a Gothic statue of the Virgin and Child on its frontage. The interior of the Chapel was much changed by the Turks, who converted it into a mosque. The coat-of-arms of Grand Master Raymond Beranger (1365 -1374) on the Chapel indicates that it I was built during his term of office and consequently that it is one of the oldest buildings in the Street of Knights. The chapel stands next to the residence of the priest, which is, now ocupied by the Italian Con-sulate. These three imposing French buildings bear witness to the power and influence of the French within the Order.

After this, an arch with a room above it is the entry to an alley at right angles to the Street of the Knights. We pass this, and immediately to our right is the **Inn of the Tongue of Pro-vence**, with the **Inn of the Tongue of Spain** to the left. The room above the archway belongs to this. Both Inns were built at the beginning of the 15th century and neither is notable for any particular exterior decoration.

Shortly after these buildings, which are the last two Inns in the Street of the Knights, a large Gothic log-gia provides a monumental end to the street. The loggia dates from the first half of the 15th century and linked the Palace of the Grand Mas-ters and the church of St John. The church, which was built in the early 14th century, was the official church of the Order. It was in good order until the middle of the last century, despite conversion into a mosque, but in 1856 a bolt of lightning struck the minaret and ignited a quantity of gunpowder which had lain in store — probably forgotten — in its cellars for many years. The explosion blew up the church, destroyed the arcade next to it and what had remained of the abandoned Palace of the Grand Masters, killing some 800 people. Fortunately, the drawings of Rottiers had preserved the design of the church, and the Italians were able to use them to build the church of the same name at Mandraki, near the Governor's Palace, now called the Church of the Annunciation. Opposite the Church of St John, at the highest point of the Castle, stood the **Palace of the Grand Masters**, a structure imposing both for its dimensions (80 metres by 75) and for the strength of its fortifications. These were so strong that even the siege of 1522 hardly damaged them. During the first years of their occupation, the Turks used the Palace as a prison, after which it was allowed to fall into ruin. The final blow was dealt by the explosion which wrecked St John's Church. However, the Italians, wishing to provide King Victor Emmanuel and Mussolini with a worthy residence when they visited the island, rebuilt it along the lines of the

The Palace of the Grand Masters, from Mandraki Harbour. The Palace was rebuilt early this century in strict accordance with the plans of the original building.

old building. It was finished in 1940. The floors are notable for their marvellous mosaics, dating from the Hellenistic and Roman periods,which were brought here from Kos. The statues which stand in the inner courtyard are also from the same periods. Greek archaeologists were brought to the brink of despair by the rebuilding of the palace, for there is considerable evidence that the famous ancient temple of Helios lies under the foundations, with its rich decorations, and this may even have been the site of the Colossus. Excavations in depth have never been conducted in this area.

As we leave the palace, Platia Kleovoulou lies to our right, and beyond this we enter a fine, wide street whose plane trees cast deep shadow even in the heat of the day. This is Odos Or-pheos. To the right, in a wall linking the interior wall of the Castle with the main wall, is the Gate of St Anthony, and after this, if we turn to the left, the impressive **d' Amboise Gate**. Iron benches between the two gates afford an opportunity to sit and rest in the shade for a while, and even — why not? — pose for a quick portrait by one of the artists to be found there.

If we turn the other way down Odós Orpheos, we will come to the Clock Tower (built after the earth-quake of 1851) which stands on the site of the north - west tower of the interior fortifications of the Collachium. From here, the wall ran downhill parallel to the Street of the Knights to the point at which it met the outer walls near the harbour. Almost none of this section of the inner wall has survived.

Time for a rest under the shade of the plane trees and a chance o watch the artists at work. Odós Orfeos.

The Suleiman Cami, at the end of Sokratous St., also known as the 'long bazaar'.

The Chora

When we leave the inner Collachium wall, we are at the top of Odós
Sokratous, the **'long bazaar'**, as the
Turks used to call it. To the left is the
Mosque of Suleiman (next to the
clock tower), standing in a fine courtyard with plane trees. It was built in
1808 in the place of an older mosque
erected in honour of the conqueror of
Rhodes, Suleiman the Magnificent.
It continues to operate as a mosque,
despite the worrying and perfectly
evident angle which its minaret now
leans at. The **Turkish library**, founded in 1794 by the Moslem Rhodian
Ahmed Hafuz, is on the other side of
the street. The library contains a fine
collection of Turkish, Arab and Per-
sian manuscripts, among which is an
anonymous chronicle of the siege of
1522. Also to be seen are two richly
ornamented Korans, one of 1412 and
one of 1540.

Odós Apollonion leads off West
from near the Suleiman Mosque.
In it stands the Byzantine-Gothic
church of St George, an elegant structure dating from the 15th century. It
was used as a medresse (a Turkish
theological school) during Otto-
man occupation, and was known as
Kurmale-Medresse (the school with
the date palm). We return to Odós
Sokratous. The first street to the right
after the Turkish library (Odós Ip-
podamou) will take us straight into
the heart of the old Turkish quarter,
which has lost almost nothing of its
medieval colour. The alleys and the
houses are very much as they were in

43

the time of the Knights. The arches beneath which the road passes every so often were added by the Turks to provide protection against earthquakes, and they add to the oriental mystery of the atmosphere. To the right of the street can be seen the chapel of Agia (Saint) Paraskevi, in a free cruciform shape. This, too, became a mosque (Takkeci Cami) during the years of Turkish rule.

The first street to the left after the mosque (Odós Archelaou) leads to Platia Arionos, where stands the **Sultan Mustafa Mosque**, built in 1765, and the public baths. These are the old **Turkish baths** (hamam), which have been restored since being destroyed in the last war. The doorman has old Turkish customs to tell of, among which is that associated with weddings: when a couple was to get married, it was the tradition that on the Friday before the wedding (which took place on Sunday) all the relatives and friends of the couple were provided with tickets for the baths, so that all could prepare themselves in a comradely atmosphere — with the two sexes separate, needless to say — for the ceremony to come.

A lane runs down from Platia Arionos between the mosque and the baths to the outdoor **Theatre of the Old City**, where performances of folk dancing are held every evening during the summer. Our street continues, coming out in Od6s Agiou Fanouriou. We turn right (to the South). The small Byzantine church of Agios Fanourios (patron saint of those searching for lost objects) is again in free cruciform style. The Turks used it first as a stable and later as a mosque (Peial el din Cami). Some fine wall-paintings have been preserved under the Turkish plaster on the walls. Immediately behind this,

Left and above: picturesque alleys in the Chora part of the Old Town.

in Platia Doriéos, is the abandoned mosque of **Redjep-Pasha**. This was built in 1588, using materials from Byzantine and Knightly times, and was, in its day, the finest mosque on the island. A fountain stands in front of it, and behind, in an archway with a vaulted roof, is the sarcophagus of Redjep Pasha himself. We return to Odós Agiou Fanouriou, one of the most picturesque in the city, and turn right, leading back to Odós Sokratous, the busy bazaar area where souvenirs of all descriptions are for sale. On the left as we enter this street is the wooden **Aga Cami** (Mosque of the Governor).

On our way down towards the harbour we pass through Platia Ippokratous, in the centre of which stands a fine fountain. Also in the square is all that remains of an important building of the Knights known as **Castellania**, of which only the south-west section stands, with a large outside staircase. The building dates from 1597 and was a commercial centre. The ground floor was used for transactions between traders, and the upper floor for the court where their disputes were tried. Only a few yards farther on is the **Marine Gate** or Harbour Gate, flanked by two bastions. It is perhaps the most spectacular of all the gates to the castle. As can be seen from engravings of past centuries, the sea used to run up to a point directly beneath the gate.

To the south of Platia Ippokratous, Odós Pythagóra leads off to the side of the **Ibrahim Pasha Cami**. Built in 1531, this is the oldest Turkish religious building to have survived. It was repaired by the Italians, who also added a new minaret.

Odós Aristotelous, which leads out of Platia Ippokratous, will take us to the old Jewish quarter and to the Square of the Hebrew Martyrs (Platia Evreon Martiron), with its attractive little fountain, decorated with rows of shells, starfish, octopuses and so on, set on blue tiles and surmounted by three large sea-horses. The name of the square is in memory of the approximately 2000 Jews, who were assembled here before being shipped to Nazi concentration camps, fromwhich only a very few

A stop for a drink in Platia Ippokratous, looking over towards the medieval building of "Castellania", isn't such a bad idea exploring the Old Town.

of them ever returned. The building whose front is on the north side of the square is the **Palace of the Admirals**, which was the residence of the Orthodox Archbishop of Rhodes before the Turkish occupation. Further along Odós Pindarou (as the continuation of Odós Aristotelous is called) are the remains of the Gothic church of **Our Lady of the City** (Sainte Marie du Bourg), the largest Catholic church in Rhodes (30 metres by 18). One part of the church lies on the left side of the road, and the other on the right.

To the south of the Square of Hebrew Martyrs, very close to the walls, is an interesting Byzantine church — the 15th century church of the Holy Trinity, better known by its Turkish name of **Dolapli Cami**. From this point on, the visitor has a choice: he can continue to wander among the narrow lanes and alleys of the old town, with their houses reminiscent of a bygone age and their half-forgotten churches and mosques, or he can return to the crowded commercial streets to increase his collection of souvenirs.

The Castle Walls

The walls of the Castle, in their final form, are an interesting example of military architecture from the period during which the cannon was making nonsense of previous theories of defensive warfare and older fortifications were proving incapable of resisting the power of gunpowder.

The contribution made by the first Knights was to repair the existing Byzantine walls. Later generations continued the improvements, and the last rebuilding was carried out under Grand Master d' Aubusson, particularly after the unsuccessful Turkish siege of 1480. This period was no-

table for its round bastions (towers) which can deflect cannon shot and were far less vulnerable than their square or rectangular predecessors. At the same time, the thickness of the wall is more than 12 metres and the moat more than 21 metres in width. The moat itself never actually contained water, being above sea level. The length of the wall, approximately four kilometres, was divided into sections, each of which was guarded by one of the Tongues.

The fountain in the centre of Platia Evreon Martiron.

The New Town

With the Turkish conquest of Rhodes in 1522, the inhabitants of the Castle changed; the Turks moved in, and only the Jews were allowed to remain. The Greek element was driven out, and permitted to live in neighbourhoods outside the walls, known by the Turkish name of «Marasia». These suburbs grew up to the South and South-East of the Castle, around spots where there had been country dwellings or churches under the Knights. It was the churches that gave the new neighbourhoods their names (St. Anastasia, St. George, St. John, St. Nicholas, etc).

During the last hundred years, still another new area of building has sprung up, the so-called «Niochóri» (new town), along the North front, and its first inhabitants were those moving to Rhodes from other nearby islands and foreigners, chiefly from Europe. This, too, was the area which the Italians chose for their modern buildings, turning it into the administrative centre of the city. Today, modern suburbs spread out to Monte Smith and the other rises to the South.

The best place to begin a stroll around the New City is **Platia Kyprou**, in the heart of the bustling and well-stocked market district. Around the square can be found the leading boutiques, jewellers, drapers and tailors, as well as almost all the banks in Rhodes. We proceed down Odós Gallias, and soon come to an extensive heptagonal building. This is the **New Market**, with its multitude of ground-floor shops (the upper floor

The New Market and Mandraki Harbour as seen from the Palace of the Grand Masters.

is occupied by offices) surrounding an open area where fruit, vegetable and meat merchants may be found and where there are plenty of coffee-shops and snack bars. Odós Averof, which runs along the side of the New Market, is the site of the RODA bus terminal, serving all the West and part of the East side of the island. A part of the Palace of the Grand Masters can be seen from here, and a garden of great beauty is where the Sound and Light display (see p. 103) is held. Near the entrance to the garden is the KTEL terminal, from which bus services to the eastern part of the island leave.

If we continue for about another 100 metres round the New Market, we will come to **Mandraki harbour**. This was the military port of ancient Rhodes, and its mouth could be shut off by chains. Now the mouth of the harbour is adorned by statues of a male and female deer – symbols of the island – which stand on columns. This was the site for the Colossus acording to a rather romantic theory. The port is used by yachts, large and small, and the local fishing vessels, and boats leave here every day for short cuises to nearby islands and to bathing places on Rhodes itself. In addition, small craft are for rent here, and the adventurous can organise and carry out their own cruises.

On the long breakwater at Mandraki stand the three medieval **windmills** which ground the grain unloaded from merchant vessels in the harbour. The main commercial harbour, known as Emporio, can be seen from here, as can the less important harbour of Akantia, to the south.

The three windmills on the pier.

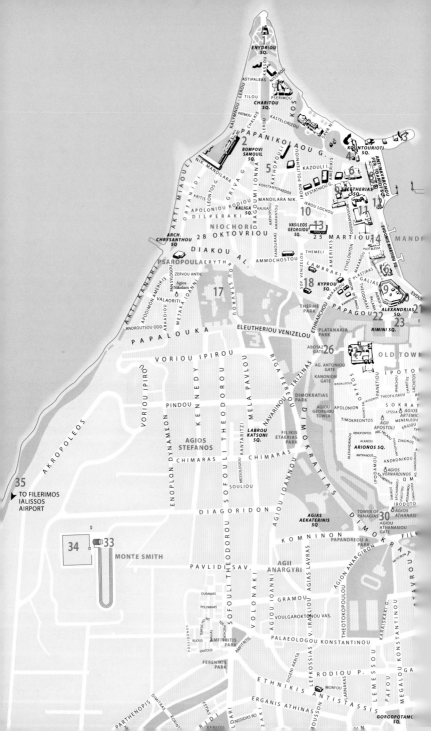

THE TOWN

1. Aquarium
2. Casino
3. Naval Club
4. Mosque of Murad Reis
5. Catholic Church
6. National Theatre
7. Fortress of St. Nicholas
8. Prefecture
9. Town Hall
10. Olympic Airways Offices
11. Post Office
12. Church of the Annunciation
13. Telephones & Telegrams
14. Courthouse
15. Windmills
16. Bank of Greece
17. Hospital
18. National Tourist Organization
19. RODA Bus Terminal
20. New Market
21. Taxi Rank
22. KTEYL Bus Terminal
23. Sound and Light
24. Gate of Freedom
25. Arsenal Gate
26. Gate d' Amboise
27. Palace of the Grand Masters
28. Commercial Harbour
29. Marine Gate
30. Gate of St. Athanasios
31. Koskinou Gate
32. New Stadium
33. Ancient Stadium
34. Ancient Theatre and Temple of Apollo
35. Road to Ixia, Filerimos, Kamiros
36. Road to Kalithea, Faliraki, Lindos

LIMENAS

28

LONA

THALASSINI GATE

AGIA AEKATERINIS GATE

AGIA AEKATERINIS GATE

AKTI SACHTOUR

PISIRODOU SQ.

KODIOU

PINDAROU

PINDAROU

THISSEOS

AICHADEF

KISTHIOU

DIMOSTHENOUS

PERIKLEOUS

NISSOU

DIONYSIOU

AGIOS PENTELEIMONOS SQ.

AKANTIA

MELINAS MERKOURI SQ.

AKANTIAS GATE

DIONYSIOU

LEONIDOU RODOU SQ.

SYMIOU

AGIA AEKATERINI SQ.

NIKASYLOU SQ.

DIONYSIOU

PROMITHEOS

AKANTIA

KARNAGIO

PRAXELOUS

AGIA TRIADA

TIRINIS

KIMONOS SQ.

KALAVRON

NAFSIKAS SQ.

NOU ARH

AFSTRALIAS

AGIOS ELEFTHERIOS

STAVROU ZISSI

LEONIDOU RODIOU SQ.

MALIARAKI MARK.

VIRONOS

KOLOKOTRONI

XANTHOUS

AGIOS GEORGIOS KATO

BEVIN ERN.

KALAVRON EM.

AFSTRALIAS

KAPODISTRIOU

MAKRIGIANNI

GIALOUROU

AGIOS GEORGIOS ANO

DIAGORA SQ.

DRADI EMA

PATRIARCHI ATHINAGORA

ZERVOU SPIROU

KANADA

KOKIDIG

AGIOS GEORGIOS KATO KORAI

AFSTRALIAS

EXPEDEFTIKON

TIAKALOU ATH

AGIOS GEORGIOU ANO

IPSILANDOU

AGIOS IOANIS

AGIOS IPSILANDOU

APOKEFALISTIS

GERONTA SQ.

MITROPOLI

KOSTARIDI SQ.

DAMASKINOU

DIAKOU

AGIOS NIKOLAOU

AGIOS NIKOLAOS

AGIOS NEKTARIOS

MITROPOLEOS

KODRIGTONOS

AGIOU GEORGIOU

MANTO MAVROGENOUS

PATRIARCHOU DIMITRIOU SQ.

PANAGOULI

MITR. I. APOSTOLOU

AFSTRALIAS

KYPRIANOU EPISK.

GIOU

NIKITARA

KANADA

TSOUSKOU CHAR

MAVRIM

VOLONAKI MIS

STAVR. AVGOUSTAKI

At the end of the mole, **the fortress of St Nicholas** dominates the harbour. This was built during the 15th century to strengthen the city's defences against Turkish attack.

The wide street along the sea-front, parallel to the quay, is the point from which all eight of the city's bus services start. Each of the routes takes about half an hour, after which the buses return to the terminus on the quay. We continue along the front in a northerly direction, passing the **Bank of Greece**, the Aktaion snack bar, the **Courthouse** and the Post-Office. Opposite the **Post Office** is the **Church of the Annunciation** (Evangelismos), built to the same plan as the Knightly church of St. John which stood opposite the Palace of the Grand Masters. This church serves as the city's cathedral. A little further along is the Prefecture, which is the former Governor's Palace, with the **Town Hall** and **National Theatre** directly opposite. All of these buildings date from the Italian occupation (1912-1943). Next to the National Theatre is the small but interesting **Mosque of Murand Reis**, with its el-

egant white minaret. Here too is the old Mohammedan cemetary, with the graves of leading Turkish citizens of the island and exiles. A circular mausoleum contains the tomb of Murad Reis himself, an admiral of Suleiman the Magnificent during the siege of Rhodes. Among the graves is also that of a Shah of Persia.

To the North, exactly opposite the mouth of the harbour, is the **Naval Club**, with facilities for young people to train in sailing, rowing, and swimming. A fine sandy beach begins at the Naval Club and stretches to the most northly point on the island, where the **Hydrobiological Institute** (Aquarium) stands. The beach continues round the point and along the other side of the cape, to the South-West, and may be used free of charge unless one wishes to hire a sun-shade or a deck-chair. The beach is most popular with tourists, who may be seen in their thousands devoting themselves to worship of the sun - a worship which is most fitting when one considers that Helios held a special place in the ancient Rhodian pantheon

Partical reconstruction of the temple of Pythian Apollo.

The "Stadium", a work from the 2nd century B.C. on Monte Smith hill.

Nearby Sights

Monte Smith

This may be reached either on foot it is less than 3 km from the town centre) or with the No.5 town bus.

The hill is named for the English admiral Sir Sidney Smith, who used the site as a lookout post for keeping watch on Napoleon's fleet, during the French war with the Turks. As stands to reason, the view is superb; we can gaze out over the town and the castle, the nearby islands and the coast of Turkey. The best time to go is in the evening, towards sunset, when the sun sinking in a blaze of crimson makes a spectacle not to be missed.

On the hill was the upper **acropolis of ancient Rhodes**. A little to the South of the hilltop is a group of important ancient remains, including, in a natural depression, the **Stadium**, which probably dates from the 2nd century BC. Much of it has been rebuilt. It is 192 metres long and 35metres wide, and it is sometimes used for concerts given by well-known Greek and foreign groups during the summer. Next to the Stadium is a small **Theatre**, reconstruction of which in white marble was made possible by the very few remaining traces of the original. It has been suggested that the Theatre was used more for the lessons in the School of Rhetoric than for actual performances of the ancient drama. Above this, the whole area was dominated by a large **Temple of Pythian Apollo**. The scanty remains of this have allowed one corner to be rebuilt. These three buildings, along with the Gymnasium which there is evidence to believe stood nearby, formed one of the main focuses of intellectual and artistic life in ancient Rhodes. Entrance to the site is free at all times.

Rhodini Park

The Park lies about 3 km from the centre of the town, alongside the road to Lindos. The Park lies in the green and shady bed of a stream, which every so often forms ponds where water-lilies may be found. This is an ideal environment for the peacocks which live and breed freely in the park and which lend it a special touch of exotic colour. It has been claimed that the Park was the site of the School of Rhetoric. The restaurant and nightclub at the entrance to the Park are only occasionally open. If we take the path which leads along the bank of the stream, a walk of about 10 minutes will bring us to a tomb dug into the rock. The tomb is mistakenly known as the Tomb of the Ptolemies. The rock has been removed outside in such a way as to form a large square base, each side of which measures 27.8 metres, and the edges of each side are decorated by 21 Doric half-columns. The tomb dates from the Hellenistic period and was restored in 1924.

ROUTES ON THE ISLAND

There are two main routes for those wishing to visit the most worthwhile sights and monuments of Rhodes. One follows the eastern coast of the island, through Lindos and down to Katavia, the most southerly village. The road is tarred, and in excellent condition with the exception of some of the southern sections.

The other route takes us along the West coast, through Ialysos and ancient Kamiros to Katavia once more. The road is tarred as far as the village of Monólithos and in good condition.

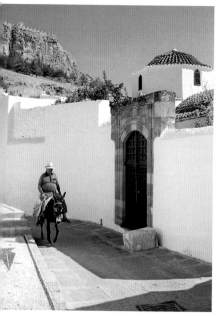

Traditional means of transport continue to be used for short distances, such as within Lindos.

In addition to these two main routes, there is a network of smaller roads linking the East and West coasts and running through all the villages in the interior of the island. All, however, are passable for motor traffic, though for reasons of safety speeds should be kept below 30-40 km per hour.

On secondary roads, especially, drivers should have their wits about them and should not hesitate to ask the way of any villagers they may come across. The locals are always willing to help, and if the visitor can get his tongue round the name of the place he wishes to go to, a flood of generally useful information will probably be produced.

Of course, all the routes which are open for four-wheeled vehicle traffic are also safe for two wheels – motorcycle or, for those whose strength and endurance is sufficient, the ordinary bicycle. Apart from private transport, all these routes are accessible by tourist coach on excursions organised by travel agencies and by public transport. The main beaches along the East coast as far as Lindos can be reached by launch, which will take the visitor in the morning and return him in the afternoon.

The southern part of the island will be of special interest to those who wish to escape from the crowds and find their own, practically deserted beach, or who wish to enjoy the Greekness of this part of the Mediterranean.

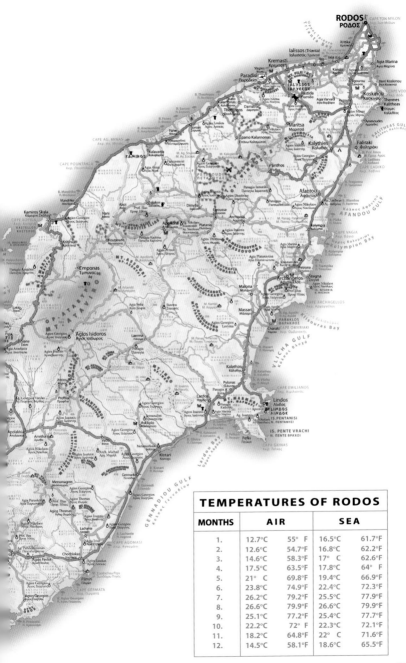

TEMPERATURES OF RODOS				
MONTHS	**AIR**		**SEA**	
1.	12.7°C	55° F	16.5°C	61.7°F
2.	12.6°C	54.7°F	16.8°C	62.2°F
3.	14.6°C	58.3°F	17° C	62.6°F
4.	17.5°C	63.5°F	17.8°C	64° F
5.	21°	69.8°F	19.4°C	66.9°F
6.	23.8°C	74.9°F	22.4°C	72.3°F
7.	26.2°C	79.2°F	25.5°C	77.9°F
8.	26.6°C	79.9°F	26.6°C	79.9°F
9.	25.1°C	77.2°F	25.4°C	77.7°F
10.	22.2°C	72° F	22.3°C	72.1°F
11.	18.2°C	64.8°F	22° C	71.6°F
12.	14.5°C	58.1°F	18.6°C	65.5°F

The East Coast

RODOS
Koskinou
Kalitheas
Faliraki
Afantou
Kolympia
Archangelos
Tsambika
Lardos
Lindos
Gennadio
Prassonissi

We leave the town along Odós Grigoriou E., in the direction of Faliraki. After five km, we arrive at the beach belonging to the village of Koskinou.. The rocky coastline is indented by small coves with sandy beaches, and it is here that some of the island's largest and finest hotels have been built. The beach is less than 500 m from the road and may be reached by turning left along one of the many little roads which run in that direction. To the right is a road which runs, in 2 km, to the village of **Koskinou**. The village is notable for the large number of houses which have interior decoration in the traditional Rhodian style and are surrounded by courtyards full of flowers.

View of Koskinou.

We continue along the coast road, which brings us, after 11 km from the town of Rhodes, to **Kalithea**. Here there were medicinal springs (no longer in operation), which a few years ago were popular with devotees of this form of therapy. There is good swimming to be had in the nearby coves.

Views of Kalithea.

The road runs south after Kalithéa, and after one km the famous beach of **Faliraki** comes in view: more than five km of golden beach and sparkling sea. The beach is backed by modern hotel units, rooms and apartments to rent, shops, restaurants, bars and all the other amenities to be found in highly-developed tourist resorts. Water sports are available. Faliraki may also be reached from the main Rhodes - Lindos road.

Views of cosmopolitan Faliraki.

Faliraki.

*The women of Afandou
are experienced rug weavers.*

One km after Faliraki a turning to the left leads, in one more km, to the quiet blue cove of **Ladikó**.

Returning to the Rhodes - Lindos road, another five km will bring us to the village of **Afántou**, on the right, with a turning on the left for Afantou beach. Afantou lies hidden amongst low hills and is surrounded by fruit orchards and olive groves, and it is one of the largest villages on Rhodes. There is a local tradition of carpet-making, which continues to be active. The long beach is clean, with pebbles in place of sand. The golf course is nearby. There are no large hotels here, but some small ones are to be found, and apartments are rented. The tavernas are notable for their good fresh fish. The bathing is definitely quieter than at Faliraki, though without the amenities.

The quiet cove of Ladiko.

Four km after Afantou we come to the hamlet of **Kolymbia**, and here we may turn left. The road leads in 2 km to the beach of the same name. There are golden, sandy coves, the most attractive of which are the two on the right as we go down.

At Kolymbia we may turn right, towards the heart of the island, and the road will lead us, after four km, to **Eptá Pigés** (seven springs), an attractive, green gorge, where springs which never dry, even in the height of summer, form a little lake. The water from this reservoir is used to irrigate the Kolymbia plain. The reservoir may be reached from the restaurant through a tunnel which is also used by the water.

Afandou beach. Who could resist the sea when it's like this?

Three km after Kolymbia a road runs to the left, passing the conical hill crowned by the **Tsambika monastery** and leading to the pretty and very popular beach of the same name. The distance from the main road is one and a half km. The sand is golden and the water clean. There are restaurants and snack bars. The road to the Tsambika monastery turns off the main road 300 m before the road to the beach. The road leads about 3/4 of the way up the green hill on, but the remainder of the path (about 15') is well worth it on foot for the wonderful view to be had, over the beaches at Afantou, Kolymbia, and Tsambika and inwards over the island as far as Mt. Atavyros. Another worthwhile way of reaching Tsambika is by one of the launches which offer one-day cruises there.

Four km further on down the road to Lindos, we come to the village of **Archángelos**. This large and picturesque village has a tradition of carpet-weaving and pottery which dates back many hundreds of years, and the local craftsmen are also famous for the goat-skin boots they turn out. Visitors planning to stay in Rhodes for more than just a few days will find the cobblers willing to make them boots on order. Near the village, on the top of a rock, are some ruins of the Castle built in 1467 by Grand Master Orsini.

Just 200 m before we enter Archangelos, a track runs off down to **Stegna** beach. This stretch of coastline is still relatively unknown to the majority of tourists, although it is a

Tsambika beach seen from high above, at the chapel of Our Lady.

great favourite with the locals. The beach itself is not as beautiful as that at Tsambika, but the cove has an attraction of its own, with the greenery which surrounds it and the excellent tavernas where good food may be enoyed in comparative peace and quiet. The beach lies some 2 km from the main road.

Four km after Archangelos, there is a turn to the left for Haraki, down on the beach three km away. This is the sea-side extension of the villages Malóna and Masari. There is a view towards Lindos and good fish tavernas. One km before we reach Haraki, another track turns to the left, and brings us, in 800 m, to a most attractive cove with goliden sand and very few visitors. Between this bay and Haráki, at the top of a cliff, stands

The potter's craft is a tradition centuries old at Archangelos.

Vlicha bay, just two kilometres from Lindos.
The long Kalathos beach starts on the extreme right.

the medieval **Castle of Feraklos**. This was one of the last strongholds of the Knights to fall to the Turks. It had been used as a detention centre for prisoners of war and Knights who committed some breach of the Order's regulations. From Archángelos, we can make a slight detour by leaving the new road and taking the old road through Malóna and Mársari. This route will bring us through the fertile Naithon valley, with its plentiful orange and mandarin trees.

Another seven km along the road to Lindos after Mársari, and we come to **Kálathos**. One and a half km later the road forks; straight ahead, and we will come to Lindos (4,5 km). The right-hand turn leads to the southern villages of the island, and that to the left leads down to the beautiful cove of **Vlichá**. Two fine new hotels stand on this beach, rooms may be rented, and there are restaurants and coffeeshops. As soon as we pass the bay of Vlichá, the imposing acropolis of Lindos comes in sight, with the village built around its foot.

Above left: The medieval castle of Feraklos.
Below: The seaside settlement of Charaki. Feraklos can be seen to the rear, left.

LINDOS

Lindos today has approximately 1000 inhabitants and is probably the most famous village in Greece, at least among foreigners. As in the case of the Old City of Rhodes, it has been declared a monument for preservation, and thus has been able to retain most of its traditional colour. It is the most popular spot for outings on the island; every day it sees an influx of thousands of foreign tourists and locals who come to admire the village and the acropolis and to swim from its marvellous beaches.

According to Homer, in the Iliad, Lindos was built by the Dorians along with Kamiros and Ialysos – this must have been about the 12th century B.C. Rhodes sent nine ships to the Trojan War, and these were probably all from Lindos. This would seem to indicate that at that time Lindos was the strongest of the Rhodian cities. The city's development, indeed, was largely a function of this sea power, for its twin harbours and its impregnable acropolis were unique in Rhodes. Even as early as the 7th century B.C. we hear reports of Lindian colonies, and the fleet cornered a large part of the trade and shipping of the Mediterranean. The Lindians were the first to draw up a code of maritime law, later known as the Rhodian law. This later became the basis for Roman maritime law, and even today forms the backbone of the law of the sea.

In the arts, the Lindians were most successful in sculpture. As the materials available in the area were not particularly suitable for sculpture in stone, the Lindans were obliged to work in bronze, bringing achievement in this to a very high point. The famous bronze Colossus of Rhodes was the work of a Lindian artist, Chares.

The city reached the height of its power in the 6th century B.C. especially in the reign of Cleoboulos who ruled for more than 40 years. Cleoboulos was regarded as one of the Seven Sages of antiquity, being the first person to have the idea that public works could be financed by collection from the citizens. There is a tradition that this was achieved by having the children of the city go from door to door singing songs written by Cleoboulos himself. This custom, known today as 'cheli-donisma', (swallow - bringing) continues to exist, and the songs that the children sing to welcome the Spring are reminiscent of their ancient counterparts, so perhaps Cleoboulos was indeed partially responsible. The money raised by these door-to-door collections was used to build the Temple of Athena, around 550 B.C., and the aqueduct which survives today at Krana and whose water runs from the spigot in the village square

When Rhodes city was founded 408 B.C., Lindos lost some of its inhabitants, and the centre for sculpture, like the shipyards, moved to the new city. But the town survived as a centre of marine trade. Rhodes lies between three continents – Asia, Africa and Europe, and it should not be forgotten that at that time ships sailed close to the coast, only by day and only in good weather. Before the sun had set each day, ships would seek a safe harbour for the night. And this was where Lindos could cash in on its position, selling supplies to the sailors and charging harbour taxes. The coming of the steamship finished off a decline which had began in the 18th century with the development of other marine centres.

*The imposing acropolis
of Lindos with the village of the slopes.*

In 1522, the Knights of St John, who had controlled trade and shipping, left the island, and the Turks who followed, having themselves little idea of or interest in trade, allowed the Lindians to organise things much as they wished. The village today contains many houses dating from the 16th, 17th and 18th centuries — which are known as the **houses of the captains**. Their architecture and decoration is unique in the Greek world. Up until very recently most of these buildings were deserted, but the money earned from tourism has enabled the locals to renovate them, under the supervision of the Archaeological Service, so as to ensure that any alterations remain within the traditional style of the town. The building of hotels is forbidden, but the Lindians have over two thousand beds available for visitors in their houses, and this is an ideal spot for those who wish to avoid the modern hotels to be found elsewhere.

The acropolis and the area which surrounds it were excavated by the Danish Archaeological School between 1902 and 1912. The oldest things found were obsidian tools dating from the Neolithic period, about 3000 B.C., and this shows how long the history of Lindos stretches back. Among the most important finds from the site, now in the Co-

One of the "captains' houses".

penhagen Museum, are two marble plaques, inscribed by Timochidas, priest of Athena, in 99 B.C. They are a list of the priests of the goddess and the other an account of the goddess's miracles, accompanied by the names of visitors to the temple and the gifts left by each. This find, known as the **Chronicle of the Temple of Lindian Athena**, states that some of the best known names of Greek mythology and history had visited the temple. Among them are Herakles, Cadmus, Danaos with his daughters, Helen of Troy and her husband Menelaos on their way back from Troy, Artaphernes, King of Persia, Alexander the Great, and many others.

The **acropolis** itself is an approximately triangular rock, 116 metres high, which is wider and lower to the North and rises through four step-ike levels to the South. The crown of the acropolis today is dominated by the walls built by the Knights. The ancient walls were much lower, and did not hide the buildings behind them.

We pass the custodian's box and climb the stairs to the first level. On the way up the steps, there are three underground water tanks and wheat storage bins dating from Byzantine times. To the left is a fine view over the bay. Statue bases, with inscriptions, stand all around; there are hundreds of these, on all four levels. The reason for this is that, especially during the Hellenistic period, it was the custom for rich visitors to the santuary to dedicate statues to Athena. Despite the number of statues that must once have stood here, very few were found during archaeological diggings.

A narrow street in Lindos, below the Akropolis.

Lindos.

It would seem that Cassius, one of the murderers of Julius Caesar, was party responsible for this, for there is a report that in 42 B.C. he removed 3,000 statues from Rhodes, and many of these must have come from Lindos.

On the first level there are two important monuments carved into the rock: an **exedra** and a **ship in relief**. In 170 B.C. the Lindians decided to honour Hagesandros, one of their sea-captains, by carving on the rock the stern of his ship (which was a form of trireme) to serve as a base for his statue, in bronze. At the bottom of the relief is a worn inscription informing us that the city of Lindos awarded Hagesandros a gold wreath. The carved exedra, which probably dates from the same period as the ship, was used as seating for what we would call today the government of Lindos. An inscription from the 3rd or 4th century A.D. informs us that Aglochartos, priest of the sanctuary of Athena, was in charge of the work of renovating the temple. The temple is known to have flourished until 396 A.D., the year in which the Byzantine Emperor ordered the destruction of all the relics of the old, pagan, beliefs. This was the time at which the Olympic Games, too, ceased to be held. The priests of Lindian Athena resisted the order, and were slaughtered.

After inspecting the ship relief and the exedra, we begin the climb up the steepest part of the acropolis. We use the stairway built by the Knights, which leads to the Castle, over the gate of which is the coat-of-arms of Grand Master d' Aubusson. The existence of this coat-of-arms shows that the castle was renovated at the end of the 15th century. A few steps of the ancient stairway are visible on the left as we ascend.

We leave the first room of the cas-

Getting to the top of the Acropolis may be tiring, but it's worth the effort.

tle and turn left through the second room, coming out in front of a row of open storerooms. On the left is another exedra, used as a base for statues, and there is a theory that this is where novices were initiated into the

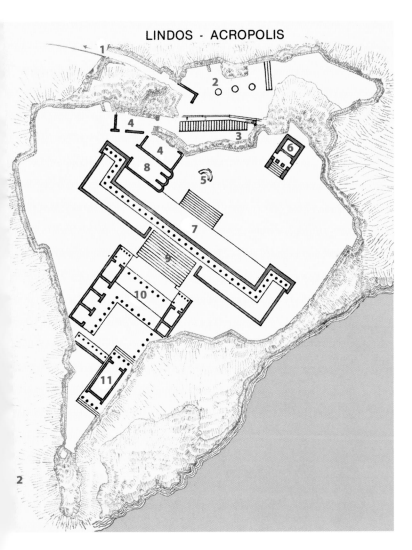

LINDOS · ACROPOLIS

LINDOS: THE ACROPOLIS

1. Street to Lindos
2. Cisterns (water tanks)
3. Exedra and ship in relief
4. Castle of the Knights
5. Exedra
6. Remains of temple, probably Roman
7. Hellenistic stoa
8. Byzantine church of St. John
9. Wide stairway
10. Propylaea
11. Temple of Lindian Athena
12. Ancient theatre

mysteries of the cult of Athena. More statues bases stand around. A little further over, to the left, can be seen the remains of what was probably a Roman temple.

The stairway to the right leads up to the third level of the akropolis Here there is a large **Hellenistic Stoa**, in the shape of a Greek P (Π). It has been said that this design was chosen because it resembled open hands welcoming the pilgrim. The Stoa dates from the end of the 3rd century B.C. and is 87 metres long, with 42 Doric columns along the front. Restoration of the Stoa and of the other ruins on the Acropolis was carried out during the Italian occupa¬tion. A problem arises here with the wind, which tends to blow down the columns which have been set upright, and so attempts are being made to save as many as possible. Next to the North - West corner of the Stoa is all that remains of the Byzantine church of St John.

The wide stairway leads up from here to the **Propylaea**. The stairway is sometimes called 'the stairs to heaven', and one does indeed have the impression that one is mounting into the clouds. At the top, on the fourth level, is the restored **Temple of Lindian Athena**. The temple is small, with a length of 22 m and a breadth of only 8, but it blends in well with the natural environment and the arrangement of the buildings on the acropolis in a way in which a larger edifice might not have done. It was the nature of the site which also forced the builders to align the temple

The Exedra and the ship in relief. In 170 B.C., the Lindians carved the stern of their most famous captain's ship in the rock to act as the base of the statue.

Part of the great Hellenistic Stoa. On the left, the temple of Athena Lindia, on the highest point of the rock.

along the unusual north-south axis. An ancient myth tells that the first temple to be built on this spot was the work of Danaos, who, fleeing from Egypt with his 50 daughters, passed through Lindos and received hospitality. Modern scholars believe that the worship of Athena began here in the 8th or 9th century B.C., without it being certain if there was a temple here at that time. In the mid-6th century, Cleoboulos either replaced an older temple or built the first one, which was then destroyed by fire in 392 B.C. The temple whose remains we see today was built in the mid-4th century on the ruins of the old building. In the centre of the temple, the base for the statue of Athena is visible. This statue was famous in its day; built of marble, wood, gold and ivory, it was reckoned a masterpiece of Greek art. Emperor Theodosios II took it to Constantinople, along with other treasures from the temple, and there it was later destroyed. The little harbour of Ayios Pavlos (St Paul) can be seen under the south corner of the rock. The harbour takes its name from the tradition that the Apostle Paul disembarked there when he came to spread the word of Christianity among the Lindians.

As we look at the harbour, **the ancient theatre** of Lindos is on our right. Some parts of the seating and the orchestra survive, carved out of the rock.

To the West of the acropolis, on the hill called Krana, is the **ancient graveyard**. Most of the shaft graves have collapsed with the passage of

time, but one, that of the Archocrates family, which dates from the 2nd century B.C., has fallen down only in the middle and will serve as an example of the magnificence of funerary architecture in Lindos.

After descending from the Acropolis and spending some time wandering through the town's narrow alleyways with their numerous souvenir shops, visitors should not neglect a visit to the **Church of Our Lady**, near the main square of the village. It was built, probably in the 14th century, on the site of an older church. Grand Master d'Aubusson renovated it in 1489 and built the belfry, on which his coat-of-arms can be seen. The church is in a free cruciform design, with an octagonal dome. Inside, the walls are covered by well-preserved wall-paintings dating from 1779, while the rood screen and the bishop's throne are marvellous examples of 17th century workmanship in wood. The church is floored with black and white pebbles in a zigzag pattern. This technique, known as the 'chochlaki' method, has its roots in the Hellenistic period and reached notable heights under Byzantium. Other examples, in various designs, can be seen all over Lindos.

A visit to Lindos is an unforgettable experience. The atmosphere of the village, whether we enjoy it fromhigh on the acropolis with its view over the ocean, the island and the two natural harbours, or in its narrow lanes with their taste of the old culture of the Aegean, provides an incomparable rest from the rush andbustle of the 'civilisation' we are all so used to.

Donkeys may be hired by the faint-hearted for the ascent of the Acropolis.

St. Paul., the second harbour at Lindos. Tradition has it that the Apostle landed here to bring Christianity to the Lindians.

We return to the fork after Vlicha bay, and take the road to the South, which will lead us into some of the least frequented parts of Rhodes. The second village we come to, **Lárdos**, is some six km farther on. This village, swamped in vegetation, boasts rooms to rent, restaurants and coffee-shops among its amenities. A track which sets off from the village winds among low green hills for five km before reaching the **Monastery of Our Lady 'Ypseni'**, an attractive white building. The church has a fine olive-wood rood-screen. Lardos Bay, another excellent beach, lies some two km from the village. The water is blue and clear, and the beach is lined with tavernas. The buildings on the eastern cape of the bay belong to the settlement of **Pefki**, where many of the inhabitants of Lindos have their summer houses.

We continue to the south, past more attractive little bays and coves. Those who wish may try following the old track, which runs directly along the shore, rather than taking the new tarred road. These coves do not usually possess restaurants or any other facilities, but they have the blessing of being free of people.

Another nine km will bring us to the fishing and holiday village of **Kiotari**, with an excellent beach and a good number of fish tavernas. Kiotari stands at the North end of an extensive bay, named Gennadi, which has miles of crystal-clear sea and pebbly beaches to offer. Every kilometre or so there are tracks running down from the main road to the beach.

Some of these tracks lead to seaside tavernas (most of them signposted) which are known for their seafood. No matter what time of the year one may visit at, it is always possible to find a spot on the beach at which the nearest people will be several kilometres away. The village of **Gennádi** is also worth a visit; it has an old church of St. George, and rooms may be rented.

Eleven km to the South of Gennadi a road runs off to the left, and leads, after one and a half km, to **Plimiri** – once more, the water is clean and the beach sandy. There is a restaurant and rooms may be rented.

Returning to the fork for Plimiri, we continue South, and another seven km will bring us to **Kataviá**, the most southerly village on the island. Near the village is the spot known as Katavos, which was the centre of the ancient community of Katabioi.

Those travelling by car or other motor transport should note that there is a petrol station in Katavia. Those with a taste for adventure can continue still further South, to Prasonisi, the southernmost cape, which lies 12 km beyond Katavia along a difficult track. **Prasonisi**, which is actually an island, is connected to the main body of Rhodes by a sandbank about 1000 m long. Depending on the direction of the wind, the sea on one side of the bank will be rough and that on the other calm.

Left: Summer resort settlement of Pefki.

Below: Kiotari with its beautiful beach.

The village of Gennadi.

Prasonisi, the southernmest tip of the island

The West Coast

RODOS

Ialissos Ixia
Paradissi   Filerímos

Kamiros   Salakos

Emponas

Monolithos

Apolakkia

As we leave the city, we pass through a small suburb consisting of identical houses which line the road. This area is known as **Kritika**, and takes its name from the Turkish refugees from Crete who were its first inhabitants in 1898.

To the right lies the **Bay of Trianda**. The north-west winds blows throughout Greece during the late summer (meltemia). However, it is also the case that the heat which can be so trying during July and August is considerably less on the West coast.

The winds have done nothing to impede the tourist development of this side of Rhodes, known as **Ixiá**, which is full of hotels large and small, restaurants, bars, snack bars, discotheques and other amenities.

Eight km out from Rhodes town we come to the village of **Triánda**, which stands on the same site as the Doric city of Ialysos in antiquity. The church of Our Lady, with a wonderful early 19th century carved wooden rood screen, is worth a visit.

Ixia.

Detail from the wooden rood screen in the Church of Our Lady at Trianda, dating from the early 19th century.

IALYSOS AND FILERIMOS

It was in 1876 that the amateur ar chaeologists Biliotti and Salzmann came across the **necropolis (grave-yard) of ancient Ialysos**, between Trianta and Mt. Philérimos. Most of the finds from the site are in the British Museum and the Louvre, and only a few are to be seen in Rhodes Museum. The most valuable finds, mostly jewellery dating from the 5th century B.C., are further evidence that the town reached its peak of prosperity at that time.

Ialysos was known throughout the ancient Greek world chiefly on account of the athletic feats of the Eratides family, and especially of Di-agoras, who won the boxing event in the Olympic Games on three occa-sions. His third victory, in 464 B.C., was celebrated by Pindar in his 7th Olympionicus. When the new city of Rhodes was built in 408 B.C., many of the inhabitants of Ialysos moved there, and the city declined and died.

The peak of **Mt. Philerimos** may be reached by turning left in Trianda and following the road for five km through a green pinewood. This was the site of the **acropolis of Ialysos**, and it was used by both Byzantines and Knights for military purposes. The Byzantine forces were besieged here in 1248 when the Genoans took the island, and it was the first site to be fortified by the Knights when they

Church of Our Lady of Filerimos.

arrived in their turn in 1306. During the great siege of 1522, Suleiman the Magnificent directed operations from the summit of the hill.

The hill itself takes its name from a monk who arrived here in the 13th century bearing an icon of Our Lady painted, as tradition goes, by St. Luke. The chapel he built later became a full-scale basilica, and on top of that, the Knights built a monastery of Our Lady in the 15th century. This was ruined by being used as a stable for the cavalry during the Turkish occupation. The Italians restored it, and even provided Cappuchine monks to reside in it. The monks returned to Italy during the War, and since then the monastery has been closed. The apse is used as a chapel of Our Lady, and is a favourite spot for romantic weddings between young Rhodians.

On our way up the ancient road which ascends the acropolis, we can see on our left the foundations of the 3rd century B.C. **temple of Zeus and Athena** and also the foundations of an **Early Christian church** with an underground font. To the left as we look at the temple is the **chapel of St George**, entirely covered within with wall-paintings of the saints, and to the right is the **Monastery of Our Lady**. As we leave the iron gate which closes off the archeological site, there is a **Doric fountain** nearby on the left. However, this cannot be visited at present, as the path is closed due to a landslide.

Returning to the main road at Tri-

The view from the top of Mt. Philerimos is particularly worth a mention. To the North lies the Bay of Trianda, with its huge hotels, and to the West the villages of Kremasti and Paradeisi.

The village of Pastida and Maritsa are visible to the South, next to the old airport, and in the distance the green slopes of Mt. Profitis Ilias and the bare crown of Mt. Atavyros.

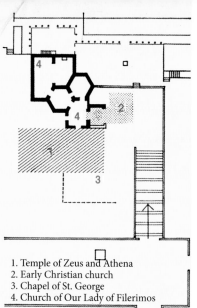

1. Temple of Zeus and Athena
2. Early Christian church
3. Chapel of St. George
4. Church of Our Lady of Filerimos

FILERIMOS

anda, we continue south-west, and after four km come to **Kremasti**. This large and lively village is notable for the survival, even in a highly tourist-conscious area, of a custom associated with the less developed parts of the Greek provinces. The village is the scene of a major religious and social event between August 14 and 23 each year, when the feast days of the church of the Dorm-ition of the Virgin (which stands to the right as we enter the village) are celebrated.

Above: Panayia church at Trianda.

Left: Doric fountain
at Filerimo (4th cent. B.C.).

Three km along the main road bring us to **Paradeisi**, where the new Rhodes international airport is situated. This, too, is a lively and charming village, whose women are especially famed locally for their beauty.

Two and a half km beyond Paradeisi a tarred road runs off to the left, and a trip of six km will bring us to the famous **Valley of the Butterflies** (Petaloudes), a green streambed which, as we shall see, has ample reason for attracting the thousands of visitors who come to see it each year. The main studies of the butterflies in the valley have been carried out by a German entomologist, Rheinhard Elger, who spent two seasons (the butterflies are present from June to September) watching them. The butterflies belong to the species *Callimorpha Quadripunctaria*. They live wherever they can find the storax (*Liquidibar Orientalis*) trees with their characteristic strong scent, pro-

The butterflies of Rhodes live and may be seen in their thousands in the valley from June to September.

duced by a kind of resin. The butterflies breed in the valley, laying their eggs there in September. The caterpillars emerge from the eggs in April spreading throughout the surrounding area, have turned into chrysalis form by May, and are full-blown butterflies by June. The heat and the smell of the storax draw them back to the valley, which they reach by travelling at night. They remain there, repeating the cycle all over again, and making the most of the coolness to be found there even on the hottest day. Low down the valley there is an attractive restaurant, built in an 'Alpine' style.

The valley of the butterflies is worth a visit even when it's not the season for the butterflies.

The area round the village of Tholos (Theologos), near the valley of the butterflies, is another attractive resort centre.

A track leads up the green hillside from the Valley of the Butterflies, and in two km brings us to the **Kalopetra Monastery**. This was built in 1784 by the exiled Greek Prince of Wallachia, Alexander Ypsilantis. The watchman serves coffee and refreshments, and the view down the valley is magnificent.

We return to the main West coast road. After three km, we come to the pretty village of **Theologos**, on our left, built on the top of a low hill. The beach here is the site of a large hotel, and there are apartments to rent, restaurants and bars.

Another three km bring us to **Soroni**, and here we can turn left into the pinewoods for a three km drive to the little **church of Agios Soulas**, where one of the most popular religious feasts on the island is held every July 29. In the afternoon there are athletic events, and horse and donkey races in a simple stadium, and in the evening there is dancing. Visitors who happen to be in Rhodes at this time may find it interesting; special buses run from the New Market for those wishing to attend.

At Kalavarda, seven km from Soroni and 30 km from Rhodes town, the road forks. The left fork leads towards the centre of the island (Mt. Profitis Ilias, the villages of Apollona and Embona, etc) and the right hand fork continues along the coast, bringing us after four km to Ancient Kámiros.

KAMIROS

The ruins of Ancient Kamiros have been called the Pompeii of Greece, but the parallel is far from complete, since Pompeii, as everyone knows, was buried in the most dramatic manner under the lava of Vesuvius, while Kamiros was gradually abandoned by its inhabitants and covered by earth with the passage of time.

The city was developed by the Dorians, as were Ialysos and Lindos. But the discovery of a Mycenean necropolis (burial ground) near the village of Kalavarda shows that in prehistoric times, before the invasion of the Dorians, the area must have been inhabited by Achaeans. In contrast to Lindos, with its tradition as a great naval power, Kamiros was largely a farming community, with figs, oil and wine as its main products. The need to export the wine and the olive oil was the stimulus for a flourishing pottery industry to grow up. It would appear that the city was at the height of its success in the 6th century B.C., insofar as this can be judged from the pottery which has been found and from the fact that it was in this century that Kamiros became the first Rhodian city to mint coins. However, when the city of Rhodes was founded in 408 B.C., the inhabitants of Kamiros began to drift away. Archaeological finds seem to indicate that a small town remained on the site into the 4th century A.D., but after that Kamiros was deserted. There

Ancient Kameiros. Buried for centuries beneath the earth.

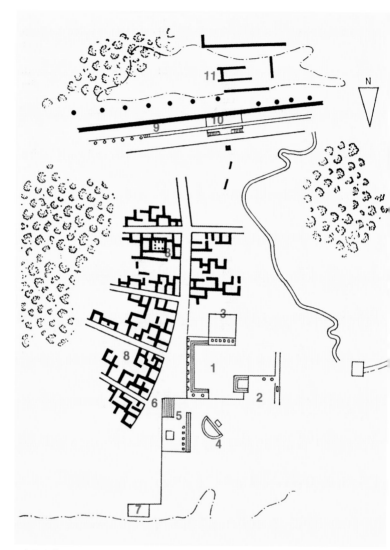

ANCIENT CAMIROS

1. Sanctuary
2. Doric Temple
3. Water Tank
4. Exedra
5. Sacrifisial area
6. Main street

7. Public baths
8. Hellenistic houses
9. Great Stoa
10. Cistern (water tank)
11. Temple of Athena

is no certainty about the reasons for which this happened, although there is a theory that successive pirate raids were responsible.

A few centuries later the whole area was given over to woods and fields, and was known to the inhabitants of neighbouring villages as 'Kambiros'.

It was this name, and the presence of some graves which villagers had turned over by chance, that led the archaeologists Biliotti and Salzmann to begin their excavations on the site. The first thing they came across was the necropolis, on the hills around the site. The finds were very rich, consisting mainly of pottery, of which the inhabitants of the ancient city were inordinately fond, filling even their tombs with it. Most of the finds were taken to the British Museum and the Louvre. During the Italian occupation of the island, work on the site was resumed, and the city was found and partially uncovered. By the time the Second World War broke out, the most important part of the city was on view.

Most of the ruins which can be seen today are from the Hellenistic and later periods and not from the Archaic period during which the town was at its height and from which we have the best finds. Kamiros was seriously damaged by earthquakes in 226 and 142 B.C.

As we enter the archaeological site, we see, directly in front of us, the **Agora** (market-place) and the **Sanctuary** of an unknown god. To the North-West of the sanctuary are the remains of a **Doric temple** of the 3rd century B.C., of which two columns have been restored. Next to this again to the North-West, is an almost geometrically perfect **Square**, with three steps on each of the East, North -East and South - East sides. Perhaps this was the spot at which the faithful sat to watch the priests performing rites in front of the temple. To the South of the square are the ruins of a **water tank** which served the needs of the market-place. In front of this is a line of restored columns.

We continue towards the steps which lead to the main street of the city, passing, on our left, a semicircular **Exedra** (rostrum), from which speeches or announcements may have been made to the people. In ancient times, the Agora was not only a mecca for those who wished to buy or sell, but also the place to which people flocked to hear the news and discuss events in their own and other areas. The Agora was the commercial, social and political centre of the ancient Greek city.

Behind the rostrum is a rectangular space enclosed by walls, which was where the altars to the various gods stood and where sacrifices were carried out. Before climbing the steps up to the main street a trial excavation into the Archaic city beneath the Hellenistic one may be seen,

To the North of the main street which bisects the site can be seen the **public baths**, constructed in the Roman fashion. There is a cistern next to them to supply water. As we climb up the road, the quarter of the private houses lies to the left and right of us. The first house on the left after the steps which lead up from the Agora has been preserved in relatively good condition; in the centre can be seen the **atrium**, the central courtyard which gave light and air to the house. Decorative columns stand round about. To the South, the columns around the atrium of another house can be seen, and still further South the ground rises more steeply to the hill on which was the acropolis.

The **acropolis** occupied a triangular and flat site on the top (120 m) of the hill. Nearly all the North side of the flat area was occupied by a **Great Stoa** (arcade), supported on two rows of Doric columns. Behind this was a line of rooms, and some archaeologists have claimed that these were shops. However it seems more likely that they were provided as ac-comodation for strangers visiting the town from other areas in order to participate in religious ceremonies. Part of the Stoa was restored by Italian archaeologists, but unfortunately the strength of a storm in 1962 proved too much for it and it collapsed. The Great Arcade was built in the 3rd century over a huge **Cistern** (water tank) which had been dug in the 6th century into the soft rock of the acropolis. This cistern could hold 600 cubic metres of rain water, which ran into it from the roofs of the buildings on the acropolis. The water was then run down into the city through an advanced system of pipes which were initially of stone and later of baked clay. The cistern passed out of use when the Stoa was built on top of it, and in order to replace it 16 smaller containers were dug under the rooms in the Stoa; these communicated underground and performed the task of collecting the rainwater.

Behind the Stoa was the temple of Athena, built at the end of the 3rd century B.C. on the site of an older temple which was probably destroyed in the earthquake of 226 B.C. The acropolis enjoys an outstanding view over the city, the sea, the smaller islands and the coast of Asia Minor.

A rest on the beach after a visit to Kamiros.

The beach of Ancient Kamiros is suitable for bathing, and there are facilities for eating. **Kámiros Skála**, 16 km to the south, was probably the port of the ancient city, though today it is a simple fishing village, with good tavernas where fresh fish may be found. A launch leaves here every morning for the 1$^{1/2}$ hour trip to the neighbouring island of Chalki.

We continue South, climbing the side of a green hill. Five hundred m after we begin to climb, a track runs off to the right, leading to the medieval **Castle of Kástellos**, which was built by the Knights in the 16h century to protect the western side of the island.

The main road continues to climb, through wonderful scenery, with an excellent view over the islands of Chalki, Alymnia, Makri, Strongyli and Tragousa. Five km further on from Kamiros Skala the village of **Kritinia**, clinging to the mountainside, comes into view. The village takes its name from its first inhabitants, who were from Crete. The myth runs as follows: Althaimenes, a grandson of King Minos of Minotaur fame, was warned by an oracle that he would kill his father, Catreas. In an attempt to avert this fate, Althaimenes took ship for Rhodes and landed here. From the top of neighbouring Mt. Atavyros he could see Crete, and so he built an altar to Zeus Atavyrios on the summit. And indeed the locals say that when the weather is good Crete can be seen, despite the fact that it lies 240 km from Rhodes. After many years had passed, Althaimenes' father wished to see him, and so he too sailed to Rhodes. But as luck would have it, they arrived at night, and the local inhabitants, taking them for pirates,

The medieval castle of Kastellos.

After octopus fishing at Kamiros Skala.

killed every one of them. Althaimenes himself killed his father, now King of Crete, and when he saw what he had done, he prayed that the earth might swallow him up and it did.

Atávyros can be seen as soon as we reach Kritinia. It is the highest peak on Rhodes (1215 m). Around the village of Embona on the lower slopes, and for some distance further up, the mountain is green with pine-forest and vineyards, while the summit itself is bare and rocky.

The road forks five km from Kritinia. The left fork leads in six km to **Embona**, while if we go straight on we will be travelling in the direction of the South end of Rhodes. Embona is interesting for those attracted by folklore, and also produces excellent

Above: the yard's a fine place to sit in the evening.
Below: the cloth is for sale, but the grapes are on the house. Embona.

The decorated interior of a house in Embona.

wine. It is among the few villages on the island where old men and women can still be seen in traditional dress. Embona can also be reached by another attractive route, from Kalavarda through Sálakos and along the sides of Mt. Profitis Ilias.

We return from Embona to the main road and continue South, through pine woods and with a panoramic view over the West side of the island and the neighbouring islets. After nine km we come to the hamlet **Sianna**, at the feet of Mt. Akramitis, second highest peak on the island (825 m). Sianna's position in the woods has made it a major producer of honey, which may be bought at the little coffee-shops in the square.

Five km on from Sianna we come to **Monólithos**, also on the slopes of

Akramitis, with a fine view back towards Atavyros and into the centre of the island. A track leading southwest out of the village and down towards the sea brings us, after one km, to the medieval **Castle of Monólithos**, built on top of a rock which gives it its name (monos lithos = single rock). It is one of the most outstanding sights on Rhodes, not so much for the remains of the castle itself, of which there are very few, but thanks to its imposing position. Inside the castle there is a chapel of Agios Pantaleimon, which probably dates from the 15th century.

The road which runs towards the sea forks after another one kilometre: the right fork will bring us to the **monastery of St George** and the left to the beach of **Fourni**, which has a beautiful combination of pinewood,

The imposing castle of Monolithos towers over the surrounding area.

sandy beach and clear water. However, those planning to spend the day there should know that there are no restaurants or other facilities on the beach.

We return to the main road. **Apolakiá** is the next village, ten km on. We are now only 17 km from Kataviá, at the South end of the island. The road, which runs close to the sea, passes between fields where wheat and melons are grown, on one side, and low sand dunes on the other. The South-West coast has a character of its own, but is not the best place for swimming due to the strong North-West winds of summer.

A turning to the left five km after Apolakia leads up through the pinewoods to the **Skiadi monastery**. The buildings date from the 18th century, and there is a view towards the coast. The monastery runs a hostel where more than 30 visitors can be accommodated. The custodian will provide coffee in the morning, to be enjoyed in the peace and aromatic tranquillity of this mountain haven. There is no stated obligation to pay for one's accommodation, but visitors are expected to contribute something towards the upkeep of the monastery.

Profitis Ilias.

From Kalavarda to Kolymbia

An interesting route through the centre of the island with its fine scenery and picturesque villages runs from Kalavarda (30 km from Rhodes town and four km before Ancient Kamiros) to Kolymbia, 24 km from the town and 24 km from Lindos, on the east coast.

The village of **Sálakos** stands eight km along this road, on the lower slopes of Mt. Profitis Ilias. The water from the local spring, called 'Nymphe, makes its presence felt in the density of the greenery and is also the main source of the water supply for Rhodes town. There is a 13h century Byzantine church.

The chapel of Profitis Ilias seen from the nearby hotel.

The Byzantine church of St. Nicholas, at Fountoukli on the slopes of Mt. Profitis Ilias.

Six km further on, the road forks. The right-hand fork leads to Embona while the left climbs up to the summit of Profitis Ilias and the hotels of Elafos and Elafina, six km away. Of these two identical Alpine-style hotels, one is always open, and is popular with Rhodian mountain-lovers during the warm summer months. Drinks are available while one is admiring the view.

The road, runs down to the East, passing through the pinewoods which supply the Rhodian deer with their habitat. Six km beyond the hotels, at **Fountoukli**, we come to the Byzantine church of St Nicholas, with interesting wall-paintings. This shady spot makes a good stopping-point, and there is a spring of refreshing water just outside the church.

Eleoúsa, a little village three km further on, was the site of the Rhodes Sanatorium, chosen for its healthy climate. Kolýmbia is another 15 km, along a surfaced road running through Epta Piges.

A solitary swim in the peace and quiet of Kolymbia.

MAKING THE MOST OF RHODES

The Archaeological Museum

As we have already mentioned in the description of the Old City, (see p.26), the Archaeological Museum of Rhodes is housed in the Hospital of the Knights, the most important and best preserved building from the period of the Knights of St. John. The museum contains a considerable amount of interesting sculpture and is especially rich in small works of art. Among the most worthwhile exhibits are the following:

— Two archaic **Kouroi** (statues of male figures) found at Kamiros. Both the statues date from the 6th century B.C., and would seem to have been made within only a few years of each other. Yet although both show a strong Egyptian influence, the later of the two shows clearly that its sculptor had a much better knowledge of anatomy and the movement of the human body.

— The famous marble funerary stele (pillar) of **Crito and Timarista,** alo found at Kamiros. This dates from the late 5th century B.C., and shows two women, mother and daughter. The mother, Timarista, is saying farewell to her daughter Crito before they part for ever. Crito, with her hair cut short in mourning, is caressing her mother's shoulder, while Timarista's right leg and arm appear to be moving slightly to the right, out of the frieze and out of the world.

— A marble **head of Helios** dating from the 2nd century B.C., found behind the Inn of Provence - not far, that is, from the highest part of the Collachium, where the temple of Helios (the sun god) is believed to have stood. The god's rich hair is sur¬rounded by holes into which metal 'sun-rays' would have fitted.

— Two fine **statues of Aphrodite.** The first, also known as Aphrodite Thalassia as the statue was found in the sea off the West beach of the town, dates from the 4th century B.C. and is larger than life-size. The goddess is shown half-clad, with a garment reaching down below her waist. The other statue shows Aphrodite naked, and is known as the Aphrodite of Rhodes. The goddess is kneeling after emerging from the sea and, her hands in a complex pose, is wringing the water from her hair. The statue, which is 49 cm high, dates from the 1st century B.C. and is made of Parian marble.

Also on view at the Museum are valuable finds from the graveyards at Ialysos and Kamiros - vessels, jewellery, scarabs, and Rhodian amphorae for the storage and transportation of liquids. There is a rich collection of coins from ancient times and from the days of the Knights, as well as Early Christian mosaics, Knightly coats-of-arms, gravestones, and so on.

Funeraly stele, Krito and Timarista
(5th century B.C.).

Above: Entrance to the Archaeological Museum.
Right: The south entrance to Kastello.

The Archaeological Museum is of great interest not only for its exhibits but also for the building itself. It is the most important and best-preserved of all the monuments to have survived from the time of the Knight of St. John.
Right: The fine marble statuette of the Aphrodite of Rhodes, in the Hall in the Museum which bears her name.

The Archaic room in the Archaeological Museum.

The Folklore Museum

This museum is housed in a building dating from the time of the Knights which occupies almost the entire South side of Argyrokastrou Square.

The well-preserved and arranged collection on display includes furniture, ceramics, embroidery, traditional folk costume and other examples of folk art from all over the Dodecanese. One room has been converted into a traditional village room as it would have looked at the time of Turkish occupation.

The Municipal Art Gallery

This is in Symis Square, over the Ionian and Popular Bank.

Kastello

The Palace of the Grand Magister. It commands the Old Town. An interior made impressive by its luxury and its wealth.

The Laocoon room with the like-named sculpture. The famous group for the 1st cent. before Christ by the Rhodiam scultors, Agesandros, Athenodoros and Polydoros.

Sports

The fine beaches of Rhodes are a paradise for lovers of sea sports, and enthusiasts of other sporting activites will find plenty to attract them, too.

SWIMMING

It is only to be expected that swimming is the most popular sport in Rhodes. There is always a choice between deep and shallow water, sandy or rocky beaches and calm, crystal-clear water or high waves. Those who think safety and pleasure on the beach lies in numbers will find things to their liking, as will those who prefer to be more or less alone. And those who hate to be separated from refreshment can use the swimming-pools at one of the big hotels. More details about specific beaches can be found in the Practical Information section.

WATER - SKIING

The eastern coast of the island, where the sea is usually calmer, makes an ideal place for water-skiing. Boats are available at all the popular beaches, and they will also provide the necessary equipment. And when the sea is calm on the West coast, water-skiing facilities will appear there, too.

WIND-SURFING

Wind-surfing becomes more popular in Rhodes every year. Windsurfers can be rented by the hour at all the popular beaches and even in the city itself. The East Coast, with its calmer waters, might be advisable for beginners, but experienced windsurfers will be sure to find the waves of the West coast a challenge worth meeting.

YACHTING

Weather conditions in Rhodes from April to October make it a yachtsman's mecca. Sailing boats of various sizes and motor-boats can be rented at Mandraki harbour. Those interested in renting small racing craft can apply to the Yacht Club, op posite the entrance to Mandraki harbour.

SUB - AQUA

Spear-fishing has many enthusiasts in Rhodes, and anyone over 18 years of age is allowed to do it. No permit is required, although it is forbidden to spear-fish near bathers. The use of underwater flash-lights at night is also prohibited. The most important prohibition of all, however, is against the use of breathing apparatus, whether for fishing or not. The full wealth of the sea-bed of Rhodes may be explored only by joining the diving school. A caique belonging to the school sets out each morning from Mandraki. One final point to remember, though it is far from unimportant, is that any antiquities found on the seabed while diving should be reported immediately to the local authorities, and any attempt to retain possession is likely to end in prosecution.

The golf course at Afandou, close to the beautiful beach of the same name.

TENNIS

Many of the large hotels outside the city have tennis courts, which are also open to non-residents who have had the forethought to make their booking in time. In the city itself, the Rhodes Tennis Club has courts near the Naval Club beach.

GOLF

There is an 18-hole golf course at Afantou, 19 km from the city. The clubhouse contains changing-rooms, lounges, a bar and a restaurant as well as a shop selling golfing equipment.

HUNTING

Only a few decades ago Rhodes was a paradise for hunters, and was especially well-known or its hare, partridges, snipe and turtle-doves. Deer hunting was always and continues to be strictly prohibited. But with more than 3,000 hunters on the island it is hardly surprising that the game has begun to disappear. The hunting season usually begins in September and ends in March. A permit is essential: more information from police stations.

Exploring the sea-bed near Kalithea.

Eating out

Good food and drink are among the many attractions of a holiday in Rhodes. The local cuisine is the result of the action of Greek imagination on a basic stock of European and eastern dishes: the most characteristically Greek elements are the use of olive oil, tomatoes, onions, garlic and a wide variety of herbs and spices. Among the most popular dishes with both Greeks and visitors are moussaka, stuffed vine leaves (*dolmádes*), meat balls (*keftedes*) and shish-kebab (*souvláki*). The locals are especially fond of fish and all the other types of seafood, but they make sure that it has been freshly caught. Fresh fish is the most expensive type of food to be had, and is sold by weight. Almost every Greek meal is incomplete without a Greek salad (*choriatiki saláta*), and this is frequently accompanied by tzatziki (side-dish made from yoghourt, garlic and cucumber) and *féta* (soft white sheep's-milk cheese). Most meals are rounded off with fresh fruit, of which the island has abundant supplies of the tastiest varieties. Among chief fruit products are apricots, peaches, water-melons, figs, grapes (all in the spring and summer) and pears, mandarins, and oranges in the autumn and winter. Prices are generally low, but will depend upon the season. Greek coffee is more or less the same as Turkish coffee. Of course, instant coffee is available everywhere nowadays, too.

Left: 'yiasou' in Greek means 'to your health', and it is the toast made when glasses are clinked. Below: eating out is twice as much fun when the setting's romantic.

131

Selecting the grapes from which the famous wine of Rhodes will be made.

The inhabitants of Rhodes are famed for their sweet tooth. Although Western-style sweetmeats are popular, the most typically Greek varieties are *baklavás* and *kataifi*. The fact that Rhodian wine was popular and highly-esteemed even in antiquity is proved by the number of amphorae containing it which have been discovered all over the Mediterranean and the Black Sea. In the Middle Ages, too, the Knights of St. John developed a taste for it and helped to spread its fame.

This tradition of producing good wine continues today. The bright sunshine and mild climate of Rhodes make it ideal for the cultivation of the vine. The main producers are the firms CAIR and EROP-EMERY, which make a wide range of popular wines. The best-known of these are 'Ilios' (dry white), 'Grand Maitre' (dry white) and 'Chevalier de Rhodes' (dry red).

Most growers make their own wine as well as selling their grapes to the industrial wine producers. Each producer makes his wine according to his own taste and recipe, of course, and after putting aside enough for his own consumption, offers the rest for sale at the island's coffee-shops ad tavernas, where it can provide a perfect accompaniment to a meal of village simplicity.

Some of the most popular Greek recipes:

Dolmádes: vine leaves stuffed with mince, rice, finely-chopped onion, herbs and spices and steamed. The dish is usually served with an egg and lemon sauce. **Keftédes:** meat balls made of mince, chopped onion, and herbs and fried in olive oil. **Moussaká:** layers of sliced potato or aubergine and mince (sometimes in tomato sauce) covered with a thick white sauce and cooked in the oven. **Yemistá:** (Stuffed vegetables): The vegetables may be tomatoes, peppers, aubergines or courgettes, and the stuffing will include mince, rice, tomatoes and herbs. Yemista are usually roasted. **Souvláki:** (Shish-kebab): pieces of veal or pork on wooden or metal spits of varying sizes, some-times with pieces of tomato, pepper and onion in between, and grilled over charcoal. **Choriátiki:** (Greek village salad): pieces of tomato, cucumber, green pepper, onion, olives, feta cheese, sometimes parsley and whatever other vegetables available and seems appropriate. **Tzatziki:** yoghourt with chopped cucumber and garlic.

On the question of drink, visitors should not forget the existence of ouzo, the Greek aperitif. This is normally drunk before a meal, and should always be accompanied by a snack (mezes) served by the establishment and included in the price, as taken by itself its consequences are highly intoxicating. When you add ice or water to ouzo its colour will change, and it will become milky- this is the effect of the aniseed which is added as a flavouring.

Time for a rest and a game of "tavli".

133

Tavernas - Restaurants
Coffee - Shops

In Rhodes it is possible to satisfy almost every gastronomic taste or whim. Establishments providing food can be divided into two main categories: tavernas (*taverna*) and restaurants (*estiatorio*). The taverna is the classic Greek eating-place. The cuisine will be uncompromisingly Greek, with an emphasis on grilled meat and fish. The appearance of the food is not so important as the creation of a casual, warm and friendly atmosphere in which Greek humour - and, if the mood comes upon them, Greek song and dance - can flourish.

The Old City is full of tavernas serving only fish and seafood. '*Meat tavernas*' are to be found in the suburbs and the nearby villages. The restaurant is a little more formal than the *taverna* and will serve so-called international cuisine in addition to Greek specialities in order to satisfy its more cosmopolitan clientele. In Rhodes town there are restaurants of various nationalities, including Chinese, Danish, and Cypriot, while for those who fancy a more romantic environment, one of the medieval buildings in the Old City has been converted into a luxury restaurant perfect for a candle-lit dinner. Then again, there is the floating restau-

On hot summer days, a table outside is the best idea.

rant in Mandraki harbour, with the Castle of the Knights, floodlit in the summer, as a backdrop. As we have already said, the Greeks are great eaters of sweetmeats, and these are to be found in the many patisseries (*zacharoplasteia*). Here traditional Greek sweets are sold side-by-side with more familiar Western-style offerings, ice-cream, coffee and drinks. The patisseries along the quay at Mandraki are very popular, and on the hot summer evenings stay open until the small hours of the morning.

The coffee-shop (*kafeneio*) is the more traditional haunt of the Greek male. Hours and hours are whiled away here over cards or backgammon (*tavli*) in a haze of cigarette smoke and political discussion. There is unwritten law against the presence villages especially, a woman in a coffee-shop will be either a tourist or the wife of the owner. The coffee-shop owner will provide small plates of snacks (tomato, olives, cheese, octopus, fried liver, etc.) to accompany glasses of *ouzo* or wine.

Although the younger people in the towns prefer the more modern environment of the cafe or bar, in the villages traditions are kept up and there is hardly a village throughout Greece, no matter how small, which does not have at least one coffee-shop. The Old City has some fine examples of

And at night, how about a drink in the moonlight?

the traditional style. In more remote parts a visit to the coffee-shop can lead to the standing of drinks and the beginning of friendships.

Night life

Apart from its historic monuments and its marvellous beaches, Rhodes also has an exciting night life to offer the visitor.

The *bouzouki* has come to be seen as the most Greek of musical instruments and is now identified with Greek popular music and entertainment. As an instrument, it has certain similarities with the mandolin. It took its final form at about the beginning of this century, when it was above all the instrument of the poorer classes of society. In the post-war period it came to be adopted by Greek society as a whole, and some of the music written for it, by composers such as Hadzidakis, Xarchakos and Theodorakis (especially with his music for the film '*Zorba the Greek*') has spread its fame beyond the frontiers of the country. Going to the *bouzoukia* is one of the ways in which the Greeks let off steam. The consumption of alcohol in such clubs is very high, and it is the custom, when a particular song or its interpretation raise enthusiasm to a climax, for plates to be broken on the dance floor in front of the singer. Prices, which are generally high, will vary from club to club according to the number and fame of the performers, and according to any other attractions which the club may have to offer.

Other dance clubs for Greek and foreign music are to be found in the town. The music will generally be live, and there is often a spot in the

The Palace of the Grand Masters, where the Sound and Light performances are given.

programme for Greek folk dances in local costumes. The audience are usually invited to come up and join the dancers, and this is a good chance to learn a few steps - which are far from being as easy as they seem! The younger members of both the local populace and the tourist population will probably prefer the lively atmosphere of a disco, and since there are tens of these in and around the town, they will have little difficulty in satisfying their demand.

Among more quiet and relaxed things to do in the evenings are the performances of folk dances held in the outdoor theatre in the Old City, the ancient tragedies and comedies put on at the Ancient Stadium, the concerts of classical music held at the National Theatre and concerts of works by modern Greek composers. The Sound and Light performances given in the verdant garden of the Palace of the Knights provide a dramatic account of the siege of Rhodes and its fall to the Turks with a fine combination of words, sound and lighting effects. Performances are given each evening in Greek, English, German, Swedish and French alternately.

The town's six cinemas concentrate on foreign films, which are subtitled rather than dubbed and may thus be enjoyed in their original language.

Last but not least is the casino which is housed in the Rodon Hotel. The games played are roulette, black-jack, and chemin de fer and there are also slot machines. Entry is permitted to those over 21 years of age, and the visitor must have his passport with him.

The bouzouki is the most popular Greek instrument, but Rhodes has interesting and varied night life suited to the tastes of all its visitors.

Cafes along the quay at Mandraki.

Shopping

A visit to Rhodes can profitably be combined with shopping-there is perhaps no other town in the world the size of Rhodes which can compete with it for variety and range. The 4000 shops in the Old and New Cities are sure to satisfy almost every demand. Rhodes has been governed since 1948 by a special customs arrangement established to assist the reconstruction of the economy after centuries of Turkish rule and three decades of Italian control. Goods are sold in Rhodes at prices which are frequently below those of their country of origin-whisky, for instance, is cheaper than it is in Britain.

In general, the cost of living in Greece-and hence in Rhodes-is considerably lower than in Western Europe. But the visitor should be careful not to buy from the first shop he enters: basic supplies and foodstuffs are subject to government price control, but consumer goods vary considerably from shop to shop.

In larger shops and supermarkets the prices are marked on the goods and bargaining is not possible, as it is in the smaller establishments and epecially in those selling souvenirs for tourists. Lower prices can often be achieved when buying a number of articles from the same shop. But Greece is no exception to the general rule that it is sometimes worth paying a little more to get better quality. As we have said above, Rhodes is an attractive shopping centre. But what are the best buys of all?

Greece has become a major centre for the international fur trade, thanks to the skills handed down from generation to generation among families of furriers in Northern Greece and particularly in the town of Kastoria. The main skill of these furriers is in the sewing together of small pieces of fur which in their countries of origin (mostly Canada and Northern Europe) cannot be used because of high labour costs. These small pieces, when sewn into larger ones, are made into excellent coats and jackets which are sold at very attractive prices. Of course, coats are also made from whole furs, but these are more expensive. The development of tourism in Rhodes has attracted many furriers to the town, each with his own workshop in which items to the measurements and taste of customers can be run up in just a few days.

The town has numerous clothing shops and boutiques, where the visitor will find the latest collections of international sportswear-Yves Saint Laurans, Pierre Cardin, Lacoste and so on-at prices little above duty-free levels. There are also tailors who make to measure, using the finest of materials, and dressmakers who can guarantee delivery within three or four days.

Greek shoes are developing an international reputation for quality and style, and are among the best buys to be made in Rhodes. Local products, too, are of particular interest: the inhabitants of Rhodes have a long tradition in silverwork, ceramics, carpet-making and embroidery. In the hundreds of shops situated in the Old City - which rather resembles one big bazaar - the visitor will find Rhodian pottery (plates, jugs, mugs etc.) decorated with traditional designs. Those curious to see how these are made can visit the potters' workshops, which spread along the roads to Lindos and Kamiros.

The villages of Afantou and Archangelos produce high-quality rugs, which can be ordered by a visit to the workshop. A visit of this type is interesting anyway, whether ordering or not, to see the way in which the rugs are woven. The shops of Rhodes also stock a wide variety of shoulder-bags, handbags, T-shirts and other articles with motifs from the island, to remind the buyer of happy holidays in Rhodes.

A characteristic example of Rhodian jewellery.

Trips to nearby islands

Rhodes is surrounded by a scatter-
ing of small islands which can make
a welcome change from its bustling
and cosmopolitan life. On these little
islands, whose chief source of income
is the sea, the simple and carefree
way of life has changed little in recent decades. If you decide to explore
them, you need only go down to the
harbour and take one of the caiques
or boats which leave from there.

SYMI

Symi is only one and a half hours
away from Rhodes by sea and there
are daily connections. It is possible to
go there in the morning and return to
Rhodes the same evening. For those
who wish to stay overnight there are
'pensions' and rented rooms.

According to Homer, Symi contributed three triremes to the Trojan
War. Symi's reputation for shipbuild-
ing survived from that remote period
down to the end of the 19th century,
when the island had some 30,000 in-

Symi.

habitants, prosperous as a result of commerce and sponge fishing. Today it builds only fishing boats and small caiques and the population does not exceed 4,000 -most of them engaged in fishing or sponge diving.

Apart from the peace and typical Aegean island beauty which Symi has to offer, there is a Byzantine castle above the town containing a church, dedicated to Our Lady, with fine murals. Near the church are the remains of an ancient temple of Athena. However, the best known sight of the island is the Bay of Panormitis with the

Monastery of St Michael, dating from the 18th century. The carved screen in church is covered with votive offerings in gold and silver.

CHALKI

Chalki is a mountainous and barren island with a certain wild beauty, lying to the West of Rhodes. Its mountains can be seen from ancient Kamiros. The island can be reached by the boat which visits all the Dodecanese twice weekly or by the caiques which leave Kamiros Skala (see p.79). The

Chalki.

trip takes about an hour and a half. Kamiros Skala can be reached by the morning RODA bus. Accommodation on Chalki is provided by rented rooms and a municipal hostel.

As on Symi, the visitor here can see what remains of a town which was economically flourishing until artificial sponges replaced natural ones. The inhabitants of these two islands and of Kalymnos are regarded as the most able sponge divers of the Aegean. Large old houses have been abandoned, while some are used by their owners, who have left the island for Rhodes, Athens or to emigrate,

only in the summer. The permanen population numbers only around 500. These are engaged almost exclusively in fishing.

The island's capital is called Nimborio and is built in the manner of ar amphitheatre around the bay of the same name. The old town - Chora stands on a hill above the harbour This was the only settlement or Chalki during the Middle Ages, because here the inhabitants could protect themselves from pirates. All that remains of the mediaeval castle, built on a steep rock, are some sections of its walls.

Symi.

USEFUL INFORMATION

Note: Every effort has been made to ensure that the information given here is as accurate as possible. However, the bublishers cannot be responsible for any omissions or mistakes due to alterations in telephone numbers, etc, after the book has gone to press.

How to get to Rhodes

By air

Via Athens
Athens is by no means a difficult place to reach, no matter what part of the world you live in. A direct or indirect flight will always be available, and there will be a range of scheduled and charter deals. Athens has two air terminals (East and West) which use the same runways. The West airport, which lies nearer the sea, serves only the international and domestic flights of Olympic Airways, and the East terminal handles foreign lines. Thus if you arrive in Athens on Olympic from abroad, all you have to do is walk a few yards along from the arrivals area and you will be in the domestic departures area. If you arrive on any other airline, you will have to change terminal; this involves a trip by coach or taxi.

To Rhodes
Rhodes is well-served by direct charter flights; it is one of the favourite destinations with tour operators world-wide, and in the height of the season as many as 50 charters may arrive on the same day. During the high season there are 6 Olympic flights between Rhodes and Athens every day. There are also flights to Karpathos (twice daily), Kos (twice daily), Herakleio in Crete (five times a week), Mykonos (four times a week) and Santorini (three times a week). Of course, flights are not nearly so frequent in the winter. If you intend to fly to Rhodes via Athens make sure your travel agent has booked you on the Rhodes flight well before you set out from your home country: in the height of the season, demand almost always exceeds supply. The Olympic Airways offices in Rhodes are at 9, Ierou Lochou St., and in Athens at 6, Othonos St., off Syntagma Sq.

By sea
Large ferry-boats ply the Piraeus-Rhodes line every day (except Sundays). A cabin will cost almost as much as the air fare, but considerable savings may be made by the hardy who are prepared to spend the night on deck or in the lounge. Those who intend to travel on deck should remember that it can be very cold, even in August. The boats usually stop at the islands of Patmos, Leros, Kalymnos and Kos, and the trip takes about 20 hours. There are also sailings to Piraeus, in about 14 hours. Since 1992 there have also been sailings to Thessaloniki. There are also ferry services — with smaller craft — from Rhodes to the other Dodecanese islands, and to Crete, but details of arrival and departure times should be checked on the spot. In addition, there is at least one departure every week for the following destinations: Limassol (Cyprus), Haifa (Israel), Alexandria (Egypt) and Ancona (Italy).

Where to stay
Rhodes has a vast variety of different kinds of accommodation at your disposal — hotels of all categories, hotel apartments, boarding -houses and rented rooms in private houses, depending on your taste and your pocket. July and August are the busiest months, and at this time it would be a mistake to come to Rhodes

without having booked accommodation in advance. If, however, this does happen, the NTOG (National Tourist Organisation of Greece) and the Tourist Police will do what they can to help you. Detailed information concerning the hotels operating in Rhodes may be obtained from the Hotel Owners' Association.

Hotels
During the last 30 years, more than 170 hotels of all types and categories have been built on the island. There are 4 de luxe hotels with a total of 2,974 beds, 44 A class with 16,308 beds, 30 B class with 4,527 beds, 65 C class with 5,879 beds, and 32 D and E class with 1,100 beds. Most of the hotels are in the town, only a few minutes' walk from both the sea and the market. However, some of the most attractive new hotels have been built outside the town, along the beaches (Koskinou, Faliraki, Lindos, Ixia, Trianda, Theologos, etc) and all these are served by frequent public transport departures to the city. Nine of the best hotels have complete conference facilities (Rhodes is an ideal place for conferences).

Hotel apartments
The demand for partially self-contained accommodation has risen to such an extent that a number of hotel apartments, as they are called, have been built in recent years. They are to be found both in the city and at the main beaches outside. They are normally for 2 - 4 persons and are equipped with kitchens where meals may be prepared.

Boarding-houses and rented rooms
Rooms may be rented both in the town and at the beaches, and Lindos is especially well-off for accommodation of this kind. There is a total of 5000 beds in private houses, some of them even inside the medieval town. The most reliable information concerning vacancies and prices is to be obtained from the Tourist Police.

Classified Practical Information

The airport
The new international airport of Rhodes is among the best in Greece. It lies 15 km away from the town, on the west coast near the village of Paradeisi. Among the services available at the airport are an NTOG office, a bank, car-hire firms, shops, a bar and a duty-free shop for those travelling abroad. Olympic Airways run buses from their town office (9, Ierou Lochou St.) to meet all their flights. Travellers should check on the departure times of these buses in advance. Those travelling as part of a group will find that the travel agency has arranged buses to take them straight to their hotels.

Antiques, antiquities and objets d' art
It is forbidden to export antiquities and works of art found in Greece, with the exception of a very few categories for which a special licence from the Ministry of Culture and Sciences is required. If a traveller is found in possession of antiquities or works of art without an export licence, the object will be confiscated

and the offender will be subject to severe legal penalties. Note too that antiques may not be bought from just anyone, but only from offically recognised antique dealers. More information may be obtained from the Rhodes Archaeological Service, in Argyrokastrou Square.

Banks and money

The main Greek banks — National, Commercial, Ionian and Popular, Credit, etc. — all have branches in Rhodes. Nearly all of them are to be found around Kyprou Sq., and currency exchange counters operate in the main tourist areas — Faliraki, Ixia, Trianda, Lindos. Banks are open Monday to Friday, 8 a.m. to 2 p.m. During the period from April to October, some of them operate in the evenings as well (5 p.m. to 7.30 p.m.) and on Saturday mornings, but only for the purposes of exchange. Visitors going to the bank to change money or traveller's cheques must remember to have their passports with them. Money and traveller's cheques may also be changed at the reception desks of hotels, but the exchange rate will be lower than that given by the banks. Inter¬nationally recognised credit cards are also accepted by the majority of shops, car-hire firms, hotels, and so on, and of course by the banks.

Beaches

The beaches of Rhodes are perhaps its major attraction. Although most of them are not organised in the proper sense of the word, changing rooms, showers, sunshades and deckchairs for hire and facilities for sea sports are often available. Entrance to the beaches is free, and payment only becomes necessary where changing-rooms, etc., are used. The beaches on the eastern coast are less prone to wind, and thus are better for swimming and sea sports. The West coast suffers, as we have said, from strong winds during the summer months, and while this makes sea sports more difficult, it does mean that it is possible to enjoy the sun without getting overheated. Apart from the well - known and popular beaches in the city and at Ixia, Trianta, Koskinou, Faliraki, Lindos and so on, the more adventurous visitor will find no shortage of deserted coves, especially along the southern coasts. For more details, see the routes on pages 47-82.

Bicycles and mopeds

Bicycles and mopeds are widely used and hired. Most of the firms which special-ise in moped rent are located in the North end of the town, close to the major hotels. It is also possible to rent bicycles and mopeds close to the hotels outside the town. They may be hired by the hour, by the day or by the week.

Camping

At present there are no organised camp sites in Rhodes apart from Faliraki camping. Rough camping is forbidden in Greece, and yet the sight of tents pitched on lonely beaches is far from an uncommon one.

Car hire

There is no shortage of car-hire firms in Rhodes, including the major interna-tional companies Avis, Budget, Hertz, Interrent and so on. Some of the larger hotels have their own cars for hire. The larger companies operate at fixed prices (depending, of course, on the size of the car), while the smaller firms and hotels are able to bargain. Prices include full insurance. The normal practice is for the car to be hired with a full tank of fuel and the difference paid on return.

Catholic services
The Catholic church of Santa Maria (on the corner of Kathopouli and Dragoumi Sts.) holds services (from April to October) at 7 a.m. on weekdays and at 8 a.m., 11 a.m. and 7 p.m. on Sundays. St. Francesca (Dimokratias St.) celebrates Mass from April to October at 8.30 a.m. on weekdays and 10 a.m. on Sundays. During the winter, both churches hold Mass only on Sundays.

Consulates
If any serious problem arises, the following consulates will be willing to assist their nationals: W. Germany: 43 Kennedy St., tel. 29 730 Great Britain: 23, 25th March St., tel. 24 963 Austria: 17, 25th March St., tel. 20 831 France: 31, Ayiou Nikolaou St., tel. 22 318 Sweden: Amerikis & I. Kazouli St., tel. 21 388 Italy: Ippoton St., tel. 27 342 Belgium and the Netherlands: 15, Hr. Polytechniou St., tel. 24 180 Finland: 93, Amerikis St., tel. 24 890.

Health
Rhodes has plenty of doctors, of all the usual varieties. Some see patients only at their private surgeries (where payment will be expected), but some also work at the State Hospital, in Erythrou Stavrou St. The hospital is open 24 hours a day for emergency cases. There are also a good number of pharmacies, one of which is always open all night.

Holidays and feast days
The following is a list of official holidays, on which all departments of the civil service and most shops are shut:
January 1 — New Year's Day,
January 6 — Epiphany.
First day of Lent (movable) — Known in Greek as 'Clean Monday'.
March 7 — anniversary of the incorporation of the Dodecanese with Greece.
March 25 — anniversary of the struggle for freedom from the Turks.
Good Friday (movable).
Easter Sunday, Easter Monday (movable).
May 1 — May Day, Of the Holy Spirit (movable).
August 15 — Dormition of the Virgin.
October 28 — anniversary of Greece's refusal to submit to an Italian ultimatum in 1940.
December 25 — Christmas Day,
December 26 — Boxing Day.

Note: The Orthodox Church movable feasts rarely coincide with those of the Western churches. The villages of Rhodes hold feasts throughout the year, at which they celebrate the day of the saint of the village church. Two of these should not be missed, if one happens to be in Rhodes at the time. The first of these is at Agios Soulas, near Soroni, on June 29. The previous day is devoted to athletic events and donkey racing in a simple stadium, with dancing in the evening. There are frequent bus departures from Rhodes town. The feast of the

Dormition of the Virgin in the village of Kremasti lasts from August 14 to 23, with dancing every evening, and during the same period the Panhellenic Handicrafts Exhibition is open in the village.

Information
Information is readily available from the locals, nearly all of whom speak at least one foreign language. But if you want to be sure, the best thing to do is to inquire at the NTOG office, at the corner of Makariou and Papagou Sts., or the Tourist Police next door. NTOG offices abroad are fully supplied with information about Rhodes and issue pamphlets.

Emergencies
Use the following telephone numbers in case of emergency: Hospital: 10625 555, Fire brigade: 199, Police: 100, Tourist Police: 27 423 We hope you never have to use it, but the Greek for "Help" is "Voithia".

Police
The major Greek tourist centres have branches of the special Tourist Police, whose duties include the inspection of hotels, restaurants and bars and service of tourists in general. Any serious complaints should be addressed to them. Officers who speak foreign languages bear the flag of the country in which the language is spoken on their uniforms. The Tourist Police headquarters are on the corner of Papagou and Makariou Sts.

Post office
The main Rhodes Post Office is at Mandraki, opposite the church of the Annunciation. It is open Monday to Friday, 8 a.m. - 8. p.m. The reception desks of most hotels sell postage stamps, and collections are made from the hotels.

Public transport
The bus network covers the island satisfactorily, and the vehicles are generally in good condition. Inside the town there are 7 bus routes, each of which takes 30 minutes to complete, with the terminus in Eleftherias Square, in front of the New Market at Mandraki. Services outside the town of Rhodes are run by two organisations: KTEYL, which serves the east coast and RODA which serves the West and part of the East. The buses of both these groups leave from the New Market at Mandraki (KTEYL from A. Papagou St., and RODA from Averof St.).

Guides
Greek guides are fully trained and those with official recognition are usually capable. They have a Union, and requests for guides in any of the European languages may be submitted to the Union offices (tel. 27 525) or the NTOG offices. Many of the travel agencies organise guided tours to the main sights of the island.

Maps
There are a number of maps of the island on the market, most of which have town plans of Rhodes city and some information. Visitors should check that the one they buy is a recent publication, as changes are frequent.

Newspapers and magazines

Most western European newspapers and magazines arrive in Rhodes a day late, and delivery can sometimes be erratic. Most of the hotels and tourist shops sell newspapers, but the best collection is to be found at the entrance to the New Market, on the quay at Mandraki.

Telephones - telegrams

Directly dialled calls can be made from Rhodes to the rest of Europe and to many other parts of the world. The head office of the Greek Telecommunications Organisation (OTE), on the corner of Amerikis and 25th March Sts., has 10 public telephones which are available 7 days a week. Opening hours are 6 a.m. -11 p.m. from November to March, and 6 a.m. - midnight from April to October.

The blue telephone boxes and the red phones to be seen all over the town are for local calls, and take 5 drachma pieces. The orange telephone boxes are for both local and long - distance calls, and accept 5, 10 and 20 drachma pieces.

Telegrams may be sent from OTE offices and from the Post Office.

Telephone rates are reduced by 30% between 8 p.m. and 7 a.m.

Passports, customs and other formalities

No visas are required for visitors from Western European and most other countries for stays of up to three months. If an extension of one's stay is desired, application must be made to the police 20 days before the expiry of the initial three - month permit. Personal belongings such as cameras, radios, cassette players, musical instruments and so on, may be brought freely into Greece, but only one of each per person. Strictly speaking, all items of this kind ought to be declared to Customs on entry, but few people bother. Duty-free goods such as cigarettes and drinks may be imported, but permissible quantities alter from time to time: check with your travel agent or an NTOG office. There is no limit to the sum in foreign exchange or traveller's cheques which visitors may bring into the country. However, sums of over the equivalent of '500 must be declared on entry, and it is forbidden to export, on leaving the country, a sum larger than that imported. It is also forbidden to export more than 4000 Greek drachmas in cash.

Weights and measures

Greece uses the metric system.
Some useful conversions and equivalents:
1 metre = 39.4 inches
1 kilometre =5/s mile
1 kilo = 2.2 Ib.
Temperature is measured in degrees Centigrade. To convert Centigrade into Fahrenheit, multiply by 9/5 and add 32. To convert Fahrenheit into Centigrade, subtract 32 and multiply by 5/9.

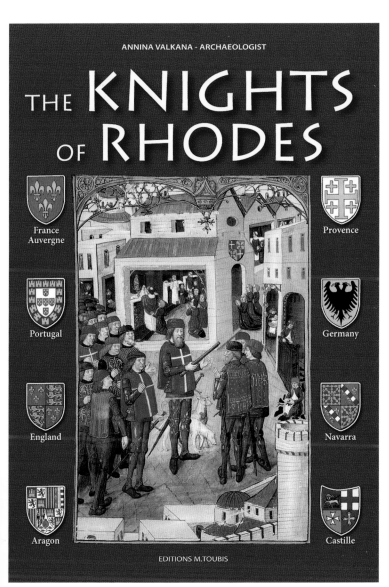

ANNINA VALKANA - ARCHAEOLOGIST

THE KNIGHTS OF RHODES

France Auvergne

Provence

Portugal

Germany

England

Navarra

Aragon

Castille

EDITIONS M.TOUBIS

Format: 17 x 24 cm, Pages: 160

HOTELS OF RODOS

The Town (0241)

Hotel	Class	Phone
GRAND HOTEL		
ASTIR PALACE	AA	26284
ATHINEON APTS	A	26112
BELVEDERE	A	24471
BLUE SKY	A	24091
CHEVALIERS PALACE	A	22781
ESAIAS APTS	A	22367
EVA APTS	A	29508
GOLDEN SUN APTS	A	63963
HELIOS APTS	A	30033
IBISCUS	A	24421
IMPERIAL	A	22431
KAMIROS	A	22591
MEDITERRANEAN	A	24661
MIRAGE APTS	A	35663
REGINA	A	22171
RIVIERA	A	22581
SIRAVAST	A	23551
SIRENE BEACH	A	30650
STEVY APTS	A	37003
VERINO	A	34881
ACANDIA	B	32251
AGLAIA	B	22061
ALEXANDROSAPTS	B	34196
ALEXIA	B	24061
AMPHITRYON	B	26880
ANGELA	B	24614
AQUARIUS	B	28107
ATHINA	B	22631
BEACH HOTEL 33	B	23857
BELLA VISTA	B	29900
CACTUS	B	26100
CITY CENTER	B	36612
CONSTANTIN	B	22971
CONTINENTAL	B	30873
CORALLI	B	24911
DESPO	B	22571
EMMANUEL	B	22892
ERODIA APTS	B	31361
ESPERIA	B	23941
EUROPA	B	22902
GEORGE APTS	B	21964
INTEUROPA	B	30648
LEFKAAPTS	B	34959
LOMENIZ	B	35748
LOTUS	B	21653
MANOUSOS	.B	22741
OLYMPIC	B	24311
PALM	B	24531
PANORAMA APTS	B	37800
PLAZA	B	22501
PRINCESS FLORA	B	62010
SPARTALIS	B	24371
SANDY COAST APTS	B	22240
SUNRISE APTS	B	30009
THERMAI	B	24351
ACHILLION	C	24604

Hotel	Class	Phone
ADONIS	C	27791
AEGAION	C	22491
AEGU	C	22789
AFRICA	C	24979
ALS	C	22481
AMARYLLIS	C	24S22
AMBASSANDER	C	24679
ASTRON	C	24651
ATLANTIS	C	24821
BUTTERFLY	C	24207
CARINA	C	22381
CONGO	C	34023
DIANA	C	24677
EL GRECO	C	24071
EUT	C	22391
EMBONA	C	24139
EMERALD APTS	C	34322
EROAPTS	C	31724
FEDRA	C	22791
FLORA	C	24538
FLORIDA	C	22111
FOUR SEASONS	C	22340
HELINA	C	24755
HERMES	C	26022
IMPALAAPTS	C	36856
INTERNATIONAL	C	24595
ISABELLA	C	22651
KAPPA STUDIOS	C	36841
KYPRIOTIS	C	35921
LYDIA	C	22705
MAJESTIC	C	22031
MANISKASAPTS	C	37412
MARIE	C	30577
MARIETTEAPTS	C	34593
MIMOZA	C	24026
MINOS	C	24041
MOSCHOS	C	24764
NAFSIKA	C	73040
NEW YORK	C	22841
NOUFARA	C	24545
CRION APTS	C	35338
PARTHENON	C	22351
PAVUDES	C	20281
PEARL	C	22420
PHILOXENIA	C	37244
RAINBOW	C	75506
ROYAL	C	24601
SARONIS	C	22811
SAVOY	C	20721
SEMIRAMIS	C	20741
ST. ANTONIO	C	24971
SUNNY APTS	C	33030
SYLVIA	C	22551
TILOS	C	24591
VASSILIA	C	35239
VENUS	C	29990
VICTORIA	C	24626
VILLA RODOS	C	20614
ANASTASIA	D	21815
ANNA MARIA	D	73685

Hotel	Class	Phone
ARIETTE	D	22490
ATLAS	D	35944
DORIAN APTS	D	31758
EFROSYNI	D	34629
EVELYN	D	2B107
KAHLUA	D	33357
MANOS	D	22620
PANTHEON	D	24567
PARIS	D	263S6
RODIAKON	D	22051
RODINI	D	27814
SEVASAPTS	D	36078
SEVEN PALMS APTS	D	36830
SOLARIS	D	30611
STAR	D	22853
XANTHI	D	24996
ZEPHYROS	D	22826
ARIS	E	23312
ILIANA	E	30251
KASTRO	E	20446
KRITI	E	21341
LA LUNA	E	25876
MARGET	E	31938
NEW VILLAGE INN	E	34937
OLD CITY	E	36951
PICADILLY	E	61937
SO NICOL	E	34561
SPOT	E	34737
STASA	E	28279
STATHIS	E	24357
SYDNEY	E	25965
TEHERANI	E	27594
GUEST HOUSES		
NIKOSTINA	A	
CAVO D ORO	B	36980
STELLA	B	24935
CAPITOL	B	74154
CASAANTICA	B	26206
INNS		
ATTALIA	B	23595
ATTIKI	A	27767
SYMI	A	23917
PENSIONS		
ATHINEA	C	23221
DORA	C	23221
LIA	C	26209
MASSARI	C	22469
ZEUS	C	23129

Faliraki (Kalithies)

Hotel	Class	Phone
APOLLO BEACH	A	85535
COLUMBIA RESORT		
HOTEL + BUNG.	A	85610
CATHRIN		
HOTEL + BUNGAL	A	85080
FALIRAKI BEACH	A	85301
LADIKO BUNGALOWS	A	85636
SUN PALACE	A	85650
ACHOUSA	B	85970
ATALANTI	B	85255

Name	Cat	Number
ERATO	B	85414
IRINAAPTS	B	86070
MODUL	B	85545
MOUSSES	B	85303
VIOLETTA APTS	B	85501
ALOE	C	86146
ANASTA APTS	C	85311
ARGO	C	85461
DIAMANTIS APTS	C	85236
DIMITRA	C	85309
EDELWEISS	C	85442
EVI	C	85586
FALIRAKI BAY	C	85645
GONDOLA	C	8S7S9
HERCULES	C	85002
IDEAL	C	85518
KOSTAS APTS	C	85520
LIDO	C	85226
LYMBERIA	C	85676
MARAN	C	86108
MATINA	C	85835
NATASA APTS	C	85507
RODANIA APTS	C	85421
SEA VIEW	C	85903
SEMELI ARTS	C	8S247
SOFIA	C	85613
STAMAT1AAPTS	C	85263
TELCHINES	C	85003
TIVOLI	C	86020
TSAMBIKA	C	85730
VENETIA	C	89612
K. SOTRILLIS APTS	D	30223
PLATON	D	85229
SAUS	D	85006
ANTONIOS	E	85100
CAMBANA	E	85281
CHRYSOULA	E	85660
DAFNI	E	85544
FAURO	E	85399
FIESTA	E	85498
IKAROS	E	85242
MARIANNA	E	85238
NEFELI	E	85658
NEST	E	85390
ODYSSIA	E	85288
PLATANOS	E	85570
REA	E	85221
RENA	E	85120
ST. AMON	E	85430
STAMOS	E	85643
STEVE	E	85233
SYNTHIA	E	85298

GUEST HOUSE

Name	Cat	Number
DANAE	A	85969
FALIRAKI CAMPING		85516

Ialyssos

Name	Cat	Number
GRECOTEL RHODOS		
IMPARIAL	AA	75000
MIRA MARE BEACH	AA	24251
OLYMPIC PALACE	AA	88755
RODOS PALACE	AA	25222
ANITA APTS	A	94258
APOLLINIA APTS	A	92951
AVRA BEACH	A	25284
BEL AIR	A	23731
BENELUX APTS	A	93716
BLUE BAY HOTEL	A	91137
BLUE HORIZON	A	93481
CARAVEL APTS	A	21843
COSMOPOLITAN	A	35373
DIONYSOS	A	23021
ELECTRA PALACE	A	92S21
ELINA	A	92466
ELIZABETH APTS	A	92656
FILERIMOS APTS	A	92510
FILERIMOS HOTEL	A	92510
GOLDEN BEACH	A	92411
GOLDEN BEACH	A	92411
IALYSOS BAY	A	91841
LATIN BEACH APTS	A	94053
MARIBEL APTS	A	94001
METROPOLITAN		
CAPSIS	A	25015
OCEANIS	A	24881
OSIRIS APTS	A	94717
PALEOS APTS	A	92431
POSEIDONIA	A	22276
RODOS BAY	A	23661
SEA MELODY APTS	A	91026
SUN BEACH APTS	A	93821
SUN BEACH No 2	A	93821
SUNNY DAYS APTS	A	35006
ALIA APTS	B	31410
ALKYON APTS	B	28637
ANIXIS APTS	B	91857
ARGO SEA APTS	B	36163
COSMOS APTS	B	94080
ELEONAS APTS	B	91376
FORUM APTS	B	94321
GALINI APTS	B	91251
KASSANDRA APTS	B	94236
LE COCO-TIERS	B	36450
LITO	B	23511
MARITINA APTS	B	35955
MATOULA BEACH	B	94251
NIKI APTS	B	94065
PACHOS APTS	B	92514
SOLEMAR	B	22941
SUMMERLANO	B	94941
SUNLAND	B	91133
SKAN APTS	B	94502
WING APTS	B	32361
BELLE ELENE	B	92173
ARLEKINO APTS	C	94255
BLUE EYES APTS	C	36797
DEBBY APTS	C	94651
EL DORADO APTS	C	94021
ELENI	C	93717
GREEN VIEW	C	91009
IXIA APTS	C	29988
MICHAEL	C	32934
MYRTO APTS	C	93400
NATALIE	C	34691
PAIMASOL APTS	C	93566
ROMA	C	24447
SUMMER TIME APTS	C	23301
SUNDAY APTS	C	91921
TASIMARI APTS	C	94380
TERINIKOS APTS	C	92174
TRIANTA APTS	C	94525
VELLOIS	C	24615
VERGINA APTS	C	94386
VILLA REA APTS	C	91522
BARBIE APTS	C	94490
SUN OF RODOS	C	
CASA MANOS	A	94355
HIPPOCAMPUS	A	36206
TAKIS APTS	A	92543
VIVIAN APTS	A	93515

GUEST HOUSES

Name	Cat	Number
EDEM	A	94284
LIZA	B	93557

PENSION

Name	Cat	Number
PEFKA	C	93388

Kremasti

Name	Cat	Number
ARMONIA APTS	A	29420
KREMASTI VILLAGE	A	92424
BLUE BAY	B	91133
SUN FLOWER	B	93893
ANSELI	C	94393
ESMERALDA APTS	C	94447
GENESSIS APTS	C	92798
KLADAKIS APTS	C	
LIOS APTS	C	94346
MARGARITA APTS	C	94254
MARITIME APTS	C	92232
MATSOUKARIS APTS	C	91277
VALENTINO APTS	C	91487
MATSIS	E	91291

Theologos

Name	Cat	Number
ALEX BEACH	A	41634
DORETTA BEACH	A	82540
HAPPY DAYS	B	41632
NIRVANA BEACH	B	41127
SABINA	B	41613
SUMMER DREAM APTS	B	41340
IFIGENIAAPTS	C	20310
IVORY APTS	C	41410
MELTTON	C	41666
ASTERIA	D	41718
STEVENSON	E	41557

Paradissi

Name	Cat	Number
VALLIAN VILLAGE	B	92309
MARAVELIA APTS	C	94210
RHODIAN SUN	C	91945
SAVELIN	C	94783

VILLA HELINA APTS	C	91175

Kalavarda

VOURAS	D	41570

Monolithos (0246)

THOMAS	A	61291

Salakos (0246)

NYMPHI	B	22206

Soroni

SILIA SORONIS	C	41026

Maritsa

MIRA MONTE	E	47244

Archagelos (0244)

ANAGROS	C	22246
ANTI SUN	C	22619
CARAVOS APTS	C	22961
HAMBURG	C	22978
KARYATIDES	C	22965
KATERINA	C	22169
MALANDROS	C	22896
NARKISSOS	C	22436
ROMANTIC	C	22749
ROSE MARIE	C	22263
SEMINA APTS	C	22210
TSAMBIKA SUN	C	22568
ARCHAGELOS	D	22230
FILIA	D	22604
PHOEBUS	D	22600

Afandou

LIPPIA HOTEL	A	52007
OASIS HOLIDAYS	A	51771
AFANDOU SKY	B	52347
GOLF VIEW	B	51935
IRIS	B	52233
RENI SKY	B	51125
SIVILIA	B	51544
STAR VIEW	B	52100
CRYSTAL	C	31687
FILIPPOS	C	51933
GOLDEN DAYS	C	52302
ROSE OF HODOS	C	22704
GOLFERS RESORT	C	27306
SCALA APTS	C	51788
KASTELLI	D	51961
NICOLIS	D	51830
ST. NICOLAS	D	51171
SEMIS	E	51525
YIANNIS	E	51565

Kolymbia

GOLDEN ODYSSEAY	A	56401
IRENE PALACE	A	51614
KOLYMBIA BEACH	A	56225
LUTANIA BEACH	A	56295
LYDIA MARIS	A	56294
MARY ANNA PALACE	A	56466
MYRINA BEACH	A	56354
NIRIDES BEACH	A	56461
ALFA	B	56411
ALLEGRO HOTEL	B	56286
AMERIKANA INTERNAT.	B	56451
DOUNAVIS	B	56212
KOALA	B	56296
KOLYMBIA BAY	B	56268
KOLYMBIA SKY	B	S6271
LOUTANIS	B	56312
MARATHON	B	56380
MEMPHIS BEACH	B	56288
MYSTRAL	B	56346
RELAX	B	56220
TINA FLORA	B	56251
TROPICAL	B	56279
KOLYMBIA STAR	B	56437
KOLYMBIA SUN	C	56213
EFKALYPTOS	E	56218

Asclepion (0244)

RODOS MARIS	A	43000
RODOS PRINCESS	A	43102
HOLIDAY SUN	B	44133
KABANARIS BAY	C	43279
KIOTARI BEACH APTS	C	43521
VILLA SYLVARA No 1	C	23997
VILLA SYLVARA No 2	C	23997

Pylona (0244)

PYLONA	D	42207

Lindos

LINDOS BAY	A	31501
LINDOS MARE	A	31130
STEPS OF LINDOS	A	31062
AMPHITHEATER	B	31351
STEPS OF LINDOS No 2	B	42262
YIOTA	B	4220S
LINDOS	B	42259
STAR OF LINDOS BAY	B	31522
FILIMON	C	44118
LINDOS AVRA APTS	C	31376
LINDOS SUN	C	314S3
PEFKOS BEACH	C	44431
SUMMER MEMORIES	C	41500
THALIA	C	44458
VLICHA SANDAY BEACH	C	42242

Gennadi (0244)

BETTY APTS	C	43020
CHRISTIANA APTS	C	43228
DOLPHIN APTS	C	41084
EVANGELOS	C	43329
GENNADI SUN APTS	C	43057
GENNADI SUN BEACH	C	43194
GOLDEN SUNRISE	C	43003
KAMIROS APTS	C	43100
MARITA APTS		43048
OLYMPOS APTS	C	43256
PANORAMA GENNADI	C	43315
SUMMER BREEZE	C	43314
TINA'S	C	43306
GENNADI BAY	B	44311
AMBELIA BEACH	B	44384

Lardos (0244)

KAMARI BEACH	A	44244
LYDIAN VILLAGE BUNG	B	44399
SUNSHINE	B	44128
NENETOS	B	44209
BEL MARE	B	44252
ILYSSIO	C	44444
LARDOS SUN BEACH	C	44203
KOSTAS	C	44141
SMARA APTS	C	44264
FEDRA	D	44213
ST. GEORGE		
LARDOS CAMPING	D	44249

Koskinou

ESPEROS VILLAGE	AA	86046
BLUE SEA	A	85582
CALYPSO	A	85455
CALYPSO PALACE	A	85621
COLOSSOS BEACH	A	85524
EDEN ROCK HOTEL	A	67067
EPSILON APTS	A	85269
ESPERIDES	A	85178
ESPEROS PALACE	A	85734
KRESTEN PALACE	A	62714
PARADISE	A	66060
PEGASSOS BEACH	A	85103
RODOS BEACH	A	85412
OLYMPOS BEACH	A	85490
SUNWING H+B	A	66140
BLUE STAR HOTEL	B	35533
CASTELLO	B	54856
KALLITHEA SUN	B	62703
LOMENIZ BLUE	B	63344
VIRGINIA	B	52041
KALLITHEA SKY	C	52703
LEMONIS APTS	C	55958
LE CHEF APTS	C	52304
Kalathos (0244)		
ATRIUM PALACE	AA	31622
KALLIGA APTS	C	21961
DANIEL	C	31101
KALATHOS SUN	D	42361
XENI	D	31171

Apolakkia (0244)

AMAUA	C	61365
SCOUTAS	E	61^51

Lachania (0244)

LACHANIA	D	43039

GREEK MYTHOLOGY

Format: 17x24 cm, Pages: 176, Photographs: 180

USEFUL EXPRESSIONS

yes / no	né / óchi
excuse me	me sinchorite
please / thank you	parakaló / efharistó
where / hear / there	poú / edó / eki
how / how far	póte / tóra
yesterday / today / tomorrow	hthés / simera / tóra
never / always	poté / pánta
good / bad	kaló / kakó
nice	oréo
up / down	páno / káto
right / left	dexiá / aristerá
in / out	mésa / éxo
how much is that	póso káni
much / a little	poli / ligo
open / closed	anichtó / klistó
hot / cold	zestó / krio
big / small	megálo / mikró
good morning	kaliméra
good evening	kalispéra
good night	kalinichta
hallow / cheers	yiásou
I want / I don't want	thélo / dén thélo
I like / I don't like	mou arési / dén mou arési
some water please	ligo neró parakaló
do you understand?	katalavénete?
I don't understand	dén katalavéno
what is this?	ti ine aftó?
can you help me?	mborite na me voithisete?
call a doctor	kaléste éna yiatró
cheap / expensive	fthinó / akrivó
what do you want?	ti thélete?
who are you?	piós isaste?
just a minute	éna leptó
I come from England	ime apó tin Aglia
I am staying at the Hotel	méno sto xenodohio
where are the toilets?	pou ine i toualétes?
where is...?	pou ine...?
how are you?	pos ise?
I am fine, thank you	ime kala efcharistó
does anyone speak English?	milá kanis Agliká?

NUMBERS

1	éna
2	dio
3	tria
4	téssera
5	pénte
6	éxi
7	eptá
8	octó
9	eniá
10	déka
11	endeka
12	dodeka
13	dekatria
14	dekatessera
15	dekapente
16	dekaexi
17	dekaepta
18	dekaocto
19	dekaenia
20	ikosi
21	ikosiena
22	ikosidio
23	ikositria
30	trianta
40	saranta
50	peninta
60	exinta
70	evdominta
80	ogdonta
90	eneninta
100	ekato
101	ekato ena
200	diakosia
300	triakosia
400	tetrakosia
500	pentakosia
600	exakosia
700	eptakosia
800	octakosia
900	eniacosia
1.000	chilia
1.001	chilia ena
2.000	dio chiliade
3.000	tris chiliade

DAYS OF THE WEEK

Sunday	Kiriaki
Monday	Deftera
Tuesday	Triti
Wednesday	Tetarti
Thursday	Pempti
Friday	Paraskevi
Saturday	Savato

MONTHS

January	Ianouarios	July	I
February	Fevrouarios	August	Avg
March	Martios	September	Septen
April	Aprilios	October	Oct
May	Maios	November	No
June	Iounios	December	Deken